T0360476

Absolute Essentials of Corporate Governance

This shortform textbook, a concise overview of the development and current state of corporate governance, provides a critical narrative on the field.

Beginning with insightful historical background, the author shows how value-adding corporate governance involves more than unthinking compliance to a recitation of statutes, regulations and principles, devoid of context. Features include basic definitions, reviews of theoretical governance problems, and a worldwide review of current governance provisions along with more detail on the UK situation. Revealing the geology of governance in the business world, the book highlights its progress set into a framework of regulation and law.

This textbook provides a brief, authoritative summary of the field for two core audiences: as a reference for specialist readers, and as an concise introduction for non-specialist readers.

Stephen Bloomfield was a member and Fellow of the Institute of Chartered Secretaries and Administrators for more than twenty-five years. After a thirty-year career in both public and private sectors, he has also lectured and led corporate governance teaching at institutions such as Ashcroft International Business School, Kingston University and London South Bank University, UK.

Absolute Essentials of Business and Economics

Textbooks are an extraordinarily useful tool for students and teachers, as is demonstrated by their continued use in the classroom and online. Successful textbooks run into multiple editions, and in endeavouring to keep up with developments in the field, it can be difficult to avoid increasing length and complexity.

This series of shortform textbooks offers a range of books which zero-in on the absolute essentials. In focusing on only the core elements of each sub-discipline, the books provide a useful alternative or supplement to traditional textbooks.

Titles in this series include:

Absolute Essentials of Strategic Marketing
Tony Proctor

Absolute Essentials of Operations Management
Andrew Greasley

Absolute Essentials of Strategic Management
Barry J. Witcher

Absolute Essentials of Green Business
Alan Sitkin

Absolute Essentials of Corporate Governance
Stephen Bloomfield

For more information about this series, please visit: www.routledge.com/Absolute-Essentials-of-Business-and-Economics/book-series/ABSOLUTE'

Absolute Essentials
of Corporate Governance

Stephen Bloomfield

Routledge
Taylor & Francis Group

LONDON AND NEW YORK

First published 2021
by Routledge
2 Park Square, Milton Park, Abingdon, Oxon OX14 4RN

and by Routledge
52 Vanderbilt Avenue, New York, NY 10017

Routledge is an imprint of the Taylor & Francis Group, an informa business

© 2021 Stephen Bloomfield

The right of Stephen Bloomfield to be identified as author of this work
has been asserted by him in accordance with sections 77 and 78 of the
Copyright, Designs and Patents Act 1988.

All rights reserved. No part of this book may be reprinted or reproduced or
utilised in any form or by any electronic, mechanical, or other means, now
known or hereafter invented, including photocopying and recording, or in
any information storage or retrieval system, without permission in writing
from the publishers.

Trademark notice: Product or corporate names may be trademarks or
registered trademarks, and are used only for identification and explanation
without intent to infringe.

British Library Cataloguing-in-Publication Data
A catalogue record for this book is available from the British Library

Library of Congress Cataloging-in-Publication Data
A catalog record for this book has been requested

ISBN: 978-0-367-55785-0 (pbk)
ISBN: 978-0-367-36159-4 (hbk)
ISBN: 978-0-429-35479-3 (ebk)

DOI: 10.4324/9780429354793

Typeset in Times New Roman
by Apex CoVantage, LLC

Contents

Introduction

This book is intended to be a short summary of the development and current state of corporate governance in the UK and other significant jurisdictions.

It aims to put these developments in context so that, even though the explanations are brief, they can be appreciated, understood and critically applied. If it is to be effective, corporate governance has to be more than an unthinking compliance to a recitation of statutes, regulations and principles, devoid of context.

It is intended for three types of potential users:

1 Those who need a brief, authoritative summary of the field but are not studying governance as a special subject, or are studying it as subsidiary to a major specialisation.
2 Specialist and non-specialist readers who require a quick source of reference for the major issues in corporate governance.
3 Those studying the subject in detail, who want a source of summarised material.

A certain amount of familiarity with the basic terms of the subject is assumed, to avoid cluttering the text with definitions. To supplement or refresh understanding, there is also a glossary of terms at the back of the book. For those who wish to know more, there are several much larger textbooks available.

Although the specific terms and descriptions used in the text are those current in the UK, the principles of governance – and the problems – are common to most jurisdictions. There is a separate chapter on corporate governance development internationally, which highlights some technical differences between jurisdictions.

Using this book

The structural and thematic skeleton of the book is as follows:

- Basic definitions and issues, necessary for understanding.
- A review of some theoretical problems that arise from these definitions and issues.
- A historical review showing the path of governance change.
- The UK's current position; where governance now stands more than a decade after the financial crisis.
- A brief and selective worldwide review of current governance provisions.
- Problems in corporate governance that are likely to arise in the future given the changing shape of companies and economies.
- Some historical examples of governance problems (in the Appendix).

While each chapter stands alone, the book is very intentionally written as a *critical* narrative explanation of corporate governance. Too often corporate governance is seen as the product of a list of reports and a later battery of laws which sprang into being in 1992 with the Cadbury Report. My experience of teaching the subject is that it *has* to be set in the context of both events and economic and political concepts in order to make consistent sense.

So, for those who have the time and the inclination and are not using the book simply to refresh their memory, the structure as written will form a summary of corporate governance progress, with successes (few) and failures (many) set into a framework of regulation and law. To use an analogy I am fond of, this method reveals the geology of the subject as opposed to just the superficial landscape.

Readers will find that I have often made reference to specific corporate governance failures in the text to illustrate a specific point, but there is a more comprehensive list of failures in the Appendix. These are often failures of the deeply flawed system of audit – which is supposed to protect shareholders' interests. Further details on all of the cases are easily found on the internet for those interested – but are not often collected together as I have done to show the frequency and magnitude of failure.

1   What is corporate governance?

- The private company/public company distinction.
- What does corporate governance try to do?
- Why does it matter?
- An explanation, a definition – and some significant criticisms.
- The major actors in governance.

From the outset it is necessary to emphasise that there is a substantial difference in most legal jurisdictions between the treatment of private companies and public companies in what is usually referred to as 'corporate governance'.

In most jurisdictions (especially those using Common Law principles) privately owned companies can organise themselves as they wish in respect of the rights of shareholders – provided that they meet statutory requirements about accounting and the payment of taxes (which are really only there to reinforce the obligation to pay taxes) – and the treatment of creditors.

Public companies – which, for simplicity (but slightly inaccurately), can be defined here as those which have shares that are freely traded on public exchanges – are usually subject to much more detailed oversight, some of which may be statutory and some of which may be contractual (in that the companies have a contract with the public exchanges to meet certain standards in terms of shareholder rights, among many other issues).

So, again for simplicity, what is commonly referred to as 'corporate governance' can be taken to mean, for the context in which it will be considered here, *the sets of rules, regulations and statutory obligations that apply to companies which have shares that are traded on public exchanges.* For the most part it is this type of company with which this book will deal, with occasional references to private companies to act as contrasts. (It should be noted, in passing, that large companies with stock market quotations for their shares form a small proportion of the total number of companies in the UK. For the most part, there is no prescription for the governance of unlisted companies beyond the bare bones of the Companies Act 2006, which is considered in Chapter 4.)

The rise in the importance of corporate governance

Insofar as it is possible to speak about 'business' as an entity, in the final two decades of the twentieth century, two significant issues both nationally and internationally out-distanced all others, at least in the Western world. Discussions about corporate affairs centred first, on *how* and, second, *for whom* businesses should be run. These two issues form the basis of the discipline of corporate governance. They are heavily intertwined with ideas about the rewards that should go to the factors of production and the risks that each assumes.

In the late 1970s and early 1980s, especially in Britain and in America, a form of capitalism had begun to develop that appeared to favour the interests of managers over those of workers, shareholders, customers and other 'stakeholders'.

To many observers it was simply *managerialism* – the rise to dominance of managers at the expense of labour and shareholders. Marxist critics of capitalism, in contrast, held the development to be a natural stage in the life cycle of capitalism. They had a point, since the characteristics had first been described in the early part of the twentieth century as *finance capitalism* – the subordination of the process of production to the accumulation of profit from money itself or 'profiting without producing'. Whatever the title, it was typified by:

1   a continual search for 'efficiencies' in the operation of businesses;
2   accelerating levels of remuneration for managers (often linked to the purported achievement of these efficiencies);
3   an increasing degree of insecurity in employment for those who were at the lower levels of management and below;
4   an increase in the rate of takeovers of businesses seen to be 'underperforming' (part of *Schumpeter's theory* of capitalism's 'creative destruction'; see Glossary);
5   'financial engineering' (see Glossary) to make certain types of capital the beneficiaries of enhanced returns;
6   the ascendancy of the accounting profession over other managerial disciplines.

In the UK by the late 1980s, after a series of scandals and controversies involving listed companies, concern was being expressed that managerialism was getting out of hand and that the balance had shifted too far in favour of managers and away from the interests of other stakeholders, particularly shareholders, in publicly owned businesses (the detailed history of this will be considered further in Chapter 3). This led to considerable public disquiet, expressed in the press and in political debate.

In 1991 the City of London Corporation and the accounting profession in the UK set up a committee of experts with the express purpose of soothing public concerns by investigating:

1   the responsibilities of executive and non-executive directors;
2   the frequency, clarity and form in which financial information should be provided (to interested parties);
3   the case for audit committees of the board;
4   the principal responsibilities of auditors;
5   the links between shareholders, boards and the auditors;
6   and any other relevant matters.

The committee's full title was '*The Committee on the Financial Aspects of Corporate Governance*' and its report was made in 1992. The committee was chaired by Sir Adrian Cadbury – the main author of its report – and came to be known as the *Cadbury Committee*. (It is important to appreciate that it was *not* a government commission, although it did receive substantial government encouragement and assistance).

The full report can be downloaded from the website of the Judge Business School at the website of the University of Cambridge. It is worth reading since it gives a clear context to many of the issues which will be discussed in this book.

The Cadbury definition

It is from this report – and the limitations of its remit – that the current definition of corporate governance stems. Although other parties have offered variants, it has been little modified over subsequent years. Unsurprisingly, it is commonly known as *the Cadbury definition*:

> Corporate Governance is the system by which business corporations are directed and controlled. Boards of directors should be responsible for the governance of their companies. The shareholders' role in governance is to appoint the directors and the auditors and to satisfy themselves that an appropriate governance structure is in place. The responsibilities of the board include setting the company's strategic aims, providing the leadership to put them into effect, supervising the management of the business and reporting to shareholders on their

stewardship. The board's actions are subject to laws, regulations and the shareholders in general meeting.

Criticisms of the definition

One of the best ways of considering the significance of the issues in corporate governance is to break the Cadbury definition down and examine it piece by piece. While it is not entirely fair to criticise the definition without reference to the more detailed findings contained in the full report, the definition has been used as the root of most subsequent work. Although this has often been helpful, it has occasionally led to blind spots, since the basic premises have not been challenged. As a consequence, despite its longevity and ubiquity, the Cadbury definition has many shortcomings.

1   *It is a product of its time.*

The committee was set up by financial institutions, including the Institute of Chartered Accountants and the Stock Exchange. It included experts in their fields nominated by those institutions – men of a certain age and position who had grown up in the system of rules, the culture and the technology they were reviewing. The composition of the committee was exclusively male.

The main method of raising large amounts of money for companies at that time was still the Stock Market. Trading in the shares of listed companies was still conducted largely by people who were known to each other, although the old distinctions of brokers (who dealt on behalf of clients and were effectively retail intermediaries) and jobbers (essentially the wholesale side of stock-dealing who 'made' prices) no longer existed, having been swept away only six years previously in the so-called London 'Big Bang', under pressure from international (principally American) banks. Electronic trading was still in its infancy; the internet did not exist in anything other than rudimentary form.

The committee deliberated for eighteen months and reviewed over 200 pieces of individual evidence, but they were constrained by the remit that the committee was given.

2   *It is a product of the remit that it worked to.*

Committees   should of course work to their remit. But the framing of the remit will also constrain what can be dealt with.

The committee was *not* expected to undertake a root and branch review of governance (a term then not in wide usage) but to confine itself to an overview. It was *not* to investigate individual cases, nor even to look outside the City or to speculate or recommend anything beyond current 'best practice'. The intention was not to rock the boat too much.

Issues such as diversity, remuneration of managers, the position and importance of workers and the position of other stakeholders (such as customers, suppliers, neighbours and the wider community) were ignored or dealt with only obliquely. Some, of course, were not yet significant issues, and their emergence later may be partly ascribed to the fact that Cadbury did *not* deal with them initially.

3   *It includes only some of the participants in the process of governance.*

The report confines itself to essentially three sets of actors: the shareholders, the auditors and the directors. Governance is limited to the interplay between that trio. As noted previously, other stakeholders are ignored.

Of the trio, the shareholders are very quickly limited to a minor role after the formation of the company and their subsequent role is only to receive historical information once it has been filtered by the directors and auditors. In the UK, the Companies Act 2006 stipulates (broadly) the form of such information.

4   *It is essentially a static definition.*

It appears to suggest that once established, the governance structures are fixed and shareholders have only the passive role of being reported to. "The shareholders role in governance is to appoint the directors and the auditors and satisfy themselves that an appropriate governance structure is in place".

Changes in governance mechanisms that might be required to deal with new issues (otherwise unforeseen) are not provided for – although it might be argued that they are implied. The only real route open to shareholders is to change the directors or sell their shares if they don't like the way things are run. So they can either "voice" their concerns; "exit" the business; or stay quiet and exhibit "loyalty", as one commentator has it (*Exit, Voice and Loyalty* by Alfred Hirschman, published in 1970).

5   *There is no consideration of ethical behaviour or an ethical framework for company activity to be measured against.*

The definition is *principle-based*, not rule-based. There is an implicit understanding that corporate behaviour will be appropriate; that shareholders, auditors and directors will all perform consistently and their behaviour will be governed by accepted norms rather than by statute.

This allows for a flexible application of principle that adjusts to change but does not deal with the reasons that the committee was established – exactly because rules and norms were being ignored or flouted. (The rules were paid lip service. The law has always found it very difficult to deal with corporate matters unless there is obvious criminality, such as fraud.)

6   *The definition appears to apply only to commercial corporations and to public companies.*

The committee's report – and the Cadbury Governance Code which grew out of it – is generally taken to apply only to listed companies (companies whose shares are *listed* – or *quoted* – on a public exchange and which can be *freely bought and sold*).

This is understandable since, as noted earlier, private companies' internal behaviour is not the general concern of the public sphere (although Sir Adrian Cadbury did exhort all companies to take note of the provisions of the Code). Yet private companies often grow up to be public companies, and for these, the bad habits of youth might well be carried over into maturity unless corrected at an early point. And of course, some public companies might own significant stakes in private companies – which are then not caught by the definition. As will be seen from a cursory examination of a financial newspaper over a few days, there are always individuals willing to push regulatory and moral boundaries – usually for their own gain.

Despite Sir Adrian's own exhortations about small companies taking note, the wording is specific to *business corporations*, presumably because – again – of the remit. But all organisations require good governance, and most have some form of trio of shareholders, directors and auditors (even though the names may be slightly different, functions will be identifiably similar). Charities, 'third sector' and public sector organisations require good governance too.

The main actors

In the trio of players identified by Cadbury, the most important are:

Shareholders

The simple status of 'shareholder' is in fact much more complicated than might be anticipated. Simply stated, shareholders are the owners of a company by virtue of having a stake in the business (represented by a valid share certificate). When this concept is unpicked, though, the position of shareholders is a lot more complicated than the simple definition suggests.

First, there is the distinction between shareholders in private companies and those in public companies. For the most part, the conceptual issues involved in being a shareholder in a private company are a lot more straightforward than they are in a public company.

It could reasonably be said that private shareholders *do* own the companies that they have a share in – although this is subject to a number of restrictions inhibiting their freedom of action to do with the company as they like, while it owes money to others. Even so, the potential for different classes of share can mean that there are different powers for different sets of shareholders depending on which class of shares they hold. Some types of share are potentially more powerful than others. In private companies the different characteristics of shares are subject to a variety of permutations of redeemability, convertibility and cumulation of dividends; these will bestow certain rights on shareholders over and above the rights of the ordinary shareholders. Some of these rights, when activated and exercised, will curtail the possible actions of ordinary shareholders. Not all these classes of shares will be entitled to vote, as a matter of course, at general meetings; but if their rights are infringed, then the shares they hold may receive a vote for the duration of that infringement.

Perhaps the most valuable right that all shareholders have – after the guaranteed right to vote at meetings (if their shares qualify them for this) – is the right for the proportion of the company their shares represent to be maintained in any subsequent share issue. This is achieved by means of *pre-emption rights* (which means the right '*to buy before*'). Shareholders in possession of this right are entitled to be offered and to buy shares in any new issue *in proportion to their existing holdings* so that their holdings are not 'diluted' by incoming money.

The share structures public companies are allowed to use are much less exotic. This is borne out of an intention to put shareholders on a roughly equal footing in terms of rights and prevent '*the oppression of minorities*'.

Some of the theoretical problems concerning shareholdings in a modern stock market will be elaborated further in Chapter 2. But individually, all that shareholders in a public company really own is the share certificate detailing the number of shares held, which they can sell or hold as they wish. The possession of these shares essentially entitles them to only one benefit – the right to receive dividends provided they hold the shares for the appropriate period while beneficial ownership is being recorded. (This is explained further in Chapter 2.)

In the case of a sophisticated share market of the type that exists in most developed economies, it really is almost impossible to conclude that shareholders 'own' the companies that they 'invest' in. The terms are largely holdovers from a simpler conceptual and legal regime and have little practical meaning for ownership.

The traditional role of stock exchanges has been overtaken by time. Only at the very first offer of shares, or in a rights issue does any money go into the company. The modern stock exchange mostly enables gamblers to bet on the rise or fall of company fortunes.

So the 'ownership' of exactly what is unclear; the money that buyers of shares pay over for the certificates are not invested in the company (except in the event of a 'new issue' of shares on to the market – perhaps through a rights issue or a flotation). The money goes to the last person to hold the certificate – the person from whom the shares were bought. Even buying shares in 'new issues' often means that the existing owners and promoters of the companies receive the proceeds of the share sales (or at least a portion of them) rather than the companies.

Shareholders are heavily circumscribed in how they can to enforce their views. Their rights to make changes are very limited – in particular about the management of the company; how they can censure the directors; what information they receive; how they receive redress; and how they can take action to prevent things they do not like. Larger shareholders may have more leverage either through informal consultation or through combining the power of their holdings in concerted action – but, effectively, not much.

Traditionalists and regulators may balk at this, but it is correct nonetheless: small shareholders, for instance, are never invited to lunches with the directors of companies, nor are they privately and discreetly consulted over pay policies for senior directors, as large pension fund holders regularly are. The leverage of small shareholders is negligible in determining the policies of a company. Their ownership in terms of their ability to move the company's policies or change directors is individually close to zero and even collectively is very limited.

Paradoxically, in stock markets most of what is loosely called 'investment' (but is really just sophisticated betting) takes place when a company makes a 'rights issue' – offering shares to shareholders in proportion to their existing holdings – and these events are often considered to be signs of corporate distress, as when a company needs extra capital to pay down a swollen debt burden, for instance. Shareholders will be asked to stump up more cash – especially if they wish to retain their share of the dividend cash generated by the company to be maintained. This is not the way shareholders expect things to go. Mostly they want to see cash flow out of a company to them, as their reward for taking the risk of buying the shares – they don't usually want to pay more money in.

Managers

The second important party – and the one that causes nearly all the problems – are *managers* (which include the directors). Most of the problems in governance arise from the role of the managers – and from the methods of rewarding managers.

The problem arises because of an issue of *agency*. This term has very specific meaning in governance and law but has become tainted recently through casual over-use of the sociological meaning. Agency in the governance and legal sense means 'to act on behalf of another' – the other being termed *principals*. Directors are therefore the agents of the shareholders – the principals – since they act on behalf of the shareholders in running the company. But one of the problems of agency is that it is nearly impossible to serve two or more principals simultaneously and satisfactorily. The shareholders as a group can be considered to be one principal – so that it is not a problem. But what happens if the director is also considered as a principal? Or the company, as a legal entity?

This problem crystallises when the question of reward for managerial services arises. The director must inevitably exercise some self-interest in the question of reward. Directors acting as profit-maximising agents for the shareholders must inevitably act as profit-maximisers for themselves in seeking the highest levels of pay. If they are not paid sufficiently, and they are good enough, then they will leave Company A to find employment with Company B, which will pay them more. If the shareholders wish to retain them, then they have to accede to the demands of the director-as-principal who is also their director-as-agent. (This issue will be looked at again in Chapter 2.)

Auditors

The third component of the governance trio consists of the auditors, who are the passive partners in the governance dance. They are employed by the shareholders to check that the annual accounts, prepared for the shareholders by the directors, give 'a true and fair view' of the business's position. Shareholders are not normally legally entitled to see any company financial statements other than the annual accounts.

Their role is nominally quite simple, protected and required (in the UK at least) by statute (s475 of the Companies Act 2006). But in practice their task throws up a number of conceptual problems, some of which are getting more and more difficult to resolve satisfactorily. At the end of 2019, their perceived role was substantially redefined in the Brydon Review.

Other actors

The Cadbury definition appears to confine the process of governance to just three participants – initially the shareholders, whose purpose is to establish the company; then the directors and auditors. The roles of these are broadly established by the definition. Perhaps most significantly of all, apart from a few warm words, the critical role of the *company secretary* was ignored:

> The company secretary has a key role to play in ensuring that board procedures are both followed and regularly reviewed. The chairman and the board will look to the company secretary for guidance on what their responsibilities are under the rules and regulations to which they are subject and on how these responsibilities should be discharged.

Instead the Committee chose to concentrate on the verification of after-the-event historical – and, consequently, necessarily inaccurate – information prepared by auditors rather than the power that could be exercised in the contemporary proper and legitimate regulation of the company by properly framed guidelines prepared by authoritative company secretaries. The role of company secretary has now been pretty much relegated to committee clerk/share registrar from its previous position of authority on governance – especially since the trend to have American-style 'General Counsel' – which smacks more of the Mafia than the Stock Market.

More up-to-date thinking expands the list of omitted parties considerably. Most authorities – academic, legal and regulatory – would now consider that there is an extensive list of *stakeholders* in any business whose numbers will include (but are not limited to):

- workers in the business;
- customers;
- suppliers;
- financiers other than shareholders;
- neighbours;
- and not least, the State.

(In fact, the Companies Act 2006 even goes so far as to recognise the interests of other parties in s172.)

Sub-categorisations of these will expand the list considerably. The concept of the stakeholders' interest in a business has given rise to the concept of *social obligations* which might be owed to these parties and consequent theories of *corporate social responsibility* (*CSR*). More recently, investing strategies which take a broader view than simple profitability or yield-based measures have also come to be known as ESG – Environmental, Social and Governance – investing.

CSR is a field fraught with problems. Much of corporate governance is concerned with issues of who is entitled to what rewards from a business – the distribution of the rewards that accrue from trading. This is difficult enough when restricted to the various parties to the enterprise under the simple Cadbury definition. For a number of reasons, it becomes much more complicated when the concepts of stakeholder interest are brought into consideration.

There are substantial legal problems in defining liabilities and obligations between such parties. Perhaps most importantly, the accounting conventions that govern company reporting have all been developed in the context of the traditional concept of shareholder ownership. They do not lend themselves to a greater illumination of other aspects of the company's activities since all the components of the income account, the balance sheet and the sources of cash are defined in terms of shareholders' needs. While these problems will be considered further in the next chapter, it should be noted that this concentration on the information priorities of the shareholders means that attempts to display different priorities are just a re-jigging of the existing information rather than any new information being elicited.

A further problem stems from the basic premises of the Cadbury definition – which leaves a lot unanswered and unresolved. It concentrated on a very limited selection of actors, mechanisms and procedures but fought shy of legal rules and obligations. It did not recognise the social ethical or moral dimension of governance (except perhaps implicitly in its foundational expectations that individuals would behave properly). The Cadbury Committee formulation is considerably flawed. Perhaps a less specific formulation might be taken as the *purpose* of corporate governance:

> Corporate governance is really about holding the balance between economic and social goals and between individual and communal goals, through legal, ethical and moral behaviour. The aim is to as nearly as possible align the interests of individuals, corporations and society.

2 Conceptual problems in corporate governance

- Who are businesses run for? Who owns the company?
- How are they run?
- The directors and the agency problem – the problem of legal personality.
- 'The controlling mind'.
- Who gets the rewards, and in what proportions?
- Actors – Who are parties to the company's activities, and how should they be ranked in importance and reward?
- Audit and financial information – What is the value of the audit?
- Competence – the timing problem of taking rewards.
- Share marketplace problems – market structural changes; market dynamics; the purpose of the stock market.
- Corporate Social Responsibility – Are companies 'citizens'?
- Unforeseen problems – technological issues; the clash of laws; concentration of market power; letter versus spirit in rule-based and principle-based systems.

The questions that form the summary at the top of this chapter are not separate and individual. They are all linked together in a complicated knot. Trying to resolve any one of them on its own will still leave the larger knot to be unravelled – and this over-arching problem is what makes corporate governance so difficult to produce codified solutions for. (It has also led to the preference, in jurisdictions which utilise the common law, to rely mostly on principle-based governance as opposed to the more prescriptive rule-based procedures often found in legal systems which use legal codes.)

Changes to any one of the individual components in an effort to resolve a problem also risk the production of unforeseen consequences that can produce further distortions elsewhere. We live in a complicated world and there are no simple solutions in corporate governance any more than in any other field of business activity.

Who are businesses run for? And how are they run?

An apparently very simple question gives rise to a very complicated area. A standard legal text will tell you that companies are run for their owners. In simple legal terms, their owners are the shareholders, so it would appear that the problem is solved.

But there are two major problems with this simplistic view. First, evidence from the real world does not accord with the theoretical statement; shareholders individually cannot make the company do what they want and may not even be able to do that if they act in concert. Furthermore, some companies also appear to be run not for the benefit of the shareholders but for the benefit of those who manage them (a very significant governance problem); occasionally some companies may be run for other purposes, as 'special interest vehicles', with objectives that may cut across those of their shareholders' interests, temporarily. A very few companies are systemically corrupt – they may have been hijacked by a specific group of shareholders who then use the company for purposes not intended, or for purposes inimical to the wider interests of the majority of shareholders.

Second, two legal constructs – one called *the veil of incorporation*, the other known as *legal personality* – complicate theoretical matters substantially.

The veil of incorporation

Companies are created by a process known as 'incorporation'. Interested individuals come together (either spontaneously or more usually as the result of someone promoting the idea of the business), subscribe a minimum amount of capital and agree certain administrative procedures (some of which are stipulated by law) which are contained in a document known as the 'Articles of Association'. They then register their agreement and the details of the company at a company registry (Companies House in the UK). The purpose of this is to distinguish the liabilities of the shareholders and the liabilities of the company. It is a means to mobilise capital by encouraging investors to involve themselves in an enterprise, with a limit to their losses (the amount that they subscribe to the capital of the company).

On incorporation – the culmination of the process of becoming a limited company – a 'veil' is dropped between the shareholders and the company, with both becoming distinct legal entities. (The 'corporate veil' is a florid legal term that originated in an 1897 case, Salomon v Salomon, where it was contended that a company and a shareholder who formed it as a contrivance to avoid debts were the same thing.) This creation of a separate entity, which owns its own assets, is the price paid by the shareholders to be removed from liability for the debts of the economic vehicle they have just created.

As a consequence of incorporation and 'the veil', they can no longer behave as if the company is their possession. Even if they decide to act in concert, they are bound by certain rules regarding the disposition of the assets of the new entity, since of course these are now no longer their assets. These rules are designed to offer some protection to creditors of the company. The veil also means that shareholders are entitled to see only certain information and have no right to demand access to the company. One of the justifications of this is that it protects all shareholders by placing them on an equal footing.

Legal personality

Incorporation creates a new legal entity – a corporate person. This new legal personality can then (a) enter into contracts, (b) sue and be sued and (c) survive its original creators. It also has certain other privileges and obligations (involving, among others, the compilation and retention of information; its capital base; and the payment of tax).

As a consequence of these two legal constructs, while it may be a convenient shorthand to say that shareholders own a company, this is effectively true only for the *complete body* of shareholders – and only in private companies. Even then, shareholders are circumscribed as to how they treat the company's assets.

How are they run?

The basic structure of company operations belongs to the era of the trading ventures of the seventeenth and eighteenth centuries, when merchant venturers came together to subscribe capital for voyages for trade in precious metals and cargo. Such very costly enterprises had to mobilise large amounts of capital from many contributors (who *subscribed* – or wrote their names – under the terms of the shareholder contract, the articles of association) and who were obviously too large in number to be actively involved in the detailed direction of the enterprise. The shareholders joined on the expectation of a *share* of the proceeds, calculated according to how much of the total capital they had contributed, properly accounted for at its conclusion. This accounting would be checked by auditors (who would listen to – or *audit* – the account of trading given by the directors) and prepare an account for submission to the shareholders. The respective roles of shareholders, directors and auditors that continue to this day were established in these ancient, large enterprises. Similarly, the concepts of limited liability for the debts of the enterprise and of contracts being entered into by the company as a legal person also arose this way.

Although companies have a legal personality, they are not, of course, able to behave in the same way as a human person. This is a problem that was recognised from the outset of incorporation.

According to Lord Thurlow, Lord Chancellor of Great Britain between 1778 and 1783, "corporations have neither bodies to be punished, nor souls to be condemned". (This description, together with other similar formulations by other leading lawyers, has significant ramifications in other areas, too, as will be shown later in considering social responsibilities.) If they have no bodies and no souls, then they can also have no minds.

If companies have no minds, then their thinking – and the execution of that thinking – has to be done for them. Clearly once the number of shareholders moves beyond some relatively small number, it becomes unreasonable to expect all shareholders to be involved in the management of the company (this is one of the practical features which might be held to distinguish a private company – usually small – from a large public company; here shareholders often play a large part in determining what a company shall do, to satisfy their objectives). To overcome the problem, the shareholders elect directors to undertake this role for them. Under UK law, all directors in all companies are subject to periodic re-election, although the terms of tenure of their posts may differ between public and private companies.

The directors

The directors form a deliberative body, the board, to take decisions collectively. The directors' decisions are recorded in minute books as matters of formal record (although the shareholders have no right to see them – at least under English law) which are there for the directors to refer to if need be – and also to justify themselves in a court of law if need be.

The board usually has a number of committees, three in most company structures: the audit committee (which deals with matters of both internal audit – a continuous, managerial task – and the completion of the external audit); the nominations committee (which deals with matters of directorial appointment and succession); and the remuneration committee (which should be composed of non-executive directors and deals with directorial and senior managerial pay).

With one exception, English law makes no distinction between directors – although there is a practical distinction between executives and non-executives. The exception is shadow directors – those individuals who act as or control other directors without being formally appointed as directors of the company. Their position is not strictly *illegal* but is what might be termed *extra-legal* in that they will be held just as liable for the consequences of their actions as those formally nominated and recorded as directors. (For external parties dealing with the company, the existence of shadow directors can provoke many practical difficulties.) Alternate directors are those who an individual may appoint (usually with the approval of the board) to stand in when the usual director is unavailable or incapacitated.

The directors are assisted in the discharge of their duties by the company secretary. Cadbury's report identified this role as

> 'The company secretary has a key role to play in ensuring that board procedures are both followed and regularly reviewed. The chairman and the board will look to the company secretary for guidance on what their responsibilities are under the rules and regulations to which they are subject and on how these responsibilities should be discharged. All directors should have access to the advice and services of the company secretary and should recognise that the chairman is entitled to strong support from the company secretary in ensuring the effective functioning of the board.'

The Companies Act 2006 requires all public companies to have a company secretary and requires the directors to make sure that the person holding the position has "the requisite knowledge and experience to discharge the functions of Secretary of the company". It does not, however, require that person to be formally qualified in the role. (Perversely, the 2006 Act weakened the position of the company secretary rather than strengthened it, by eliminating the obligation to have a designated role for small companies – although the tasks still have to be discharged – and removing the qualification requirement for large ones.)

The directors are required to produce statements of account properly prepared for submission to the shareholders for their scrutiny. The auditors are required to attest that *at the date they signed the accounts* they represented a true and fair view of the situation of the company. One day later and this situation may not hold true. From it is evident that the responsibility for both the accounts and the financial health of the company belongs to the directors, not to the auditors.

The directors and the agency problem

One of the problems with the issue of 'agency' is that the law holds that an agent cannot successfully serve two principals on the same matter. Inevitably, time – if nothing else – dictates that the interests of one principal will have to be preferred over those of another.

The director is held to be (in the purest form of company structure) the agent of the shareholders. But shareholders do not necessarily have homogenous interests, and the interest of the director in acting for himself or herself, in the matter of pay for example, will not necessarily accord with the interests of the shareholders. Directors are under a duty to avoid a conflict of interest (as will be considered in the next chapter when their duties are outlined), but such requirements are blunt and do not apply to issues of pay. At the root of many corporate scandals are issues of agency in respect of pay. The Thomas Cook collapse is an example of directors acting as agents in their own capacity and that behaviour conflicting with the interests of the shareholders. Any accounting device (and there are many) which favours directorial reward over shareholder returns falls into the same category. Some of the proposals which supposedly 'align share-holders' interests' with directorial pay are clearly conflicts of the agent's responsibility.

The shareholders have to trust the directors to work diligently and pursue the best interests of the company. This immediately gives rise to another problem: Who is to blame when things go wrong? That is not so much of a problem when the mistakes made are ones of strategy – costly though they may be. Theoretically the solution is for the shareholders to sack the director or directors and appoint new ones (although this is not so easy in a public company).

What happens when a company's actions break the law – perhaps when an effluent discharge pollutes a watercourse? Or if a faulty product results in the death or injury of a customer? Or if a worker is killed through unsafe working practices? Or, even more insidiously, when a service is offered to customers which is known by managers to be unethical but is undertaken nonetheless in the pursuit of profit? These issues have partly to do with the 'agency problem' but also involve issues of 'the controlling mind', which is considered later in this chapter.

Who gets the rewards and in what proportions?

Shareholders establish a company, by incorporation, for some economic purpose. That purpose is usually to increase their own wealth – to make money by supplying some form of need, expressed in the form of effective demand. They cannot usually do this themselves independently, so they band together and appoint directors who act as their agents in bringing together the resources of production and producing goods or services. Good agents cost money, and the best agents cost more money than the ordinary ones. Good resources of production – labour, land, machinery – also cost money, and with a similar premium for the best.

The way in which these factors of production are rewarded is a central problem in governance, and one from which most of the others spring. The subject and its ramifications are too extensive to analyse with any depth in a book like this. Some of the major issues are outlined and the reader might like to consult specialist texts noted in the Appendix on further reading for more detail.

The agency factor complicates the interactions of shareholders and directors. In terms of direct rewards, shareholders have often sought to flush out the problems of the agency relationship by offering managers bonuses for performance that enhances the shareholders' wealth, thus linking one with the other. This has led to a cultural shorthand – 'the bonus culture' – which signifies both a backfire in the way that the measures are supposed to work and popular scepticism of the mechanism itself.

There are a number of problems with bonus systems – not least that the managers are usually the architects and designers of the bonus system and are advised by professional specialists who are themselves dependent upon growing the overall value of the managerial cadre so that they can charge more for their own services (since the managers are their direct clients rather than the shareholders).

Second, one of the ways in which managers can enhance the performance of the company (and inflate their own perceived performance) is to hold down the rewards going to the other factors. The most costly factor of production in most businesses is usually the cost of employees. Only so much can be done about the costs of land and machinery (moving to a cheaper location, which may have its own drawbacks; using cheaper or less efficient machinery, which might produce temporary boosts but at long-term disadvantage). Depressing wages (the reward to labour), both individually and collectively, has the beneficial effect of allowing managers to achieve a treble score – reduced costs bring enhanced profits; enhanced profits push their own bonuses up – and usually without too much short- and medium-term disadvantage. Then, because shareholders are pleased with the result and accord managers the accolades of being skilful when they merely carry sharp knives, lauded managers can then find new employers willing to pay them more for their supposed skills. Problems that occur after they have left caused by under-manning or workforce unhappiness are then their successors' problems.

There may also be problems with the way that shareholders perceive the increase in their own wealth on which the remuneration and rewards of other factors are based. Are they looking for the value of the company to increase in terms of market capitalisation (which can be a complicated relationship between the price/earnings ratio of a company, the supposed 'quality' of earnings and the perceptions of commentators)? Are they looking for increased dividends – and regular sustainable increases? Or increased turnover, signifying growth which may produce even more enhanced dividends in the future? Some shareholders may want one of these in preference to other measures. It will be left to the directors (as the shareholders' agents) to devise a bonus structure that supposedly addresses these issues. Complicated systems which attempt to cover them all will inevitably result in seriously distorted results. Simple systems which focus on only one measure are susceptible to manipulation.

Rewards and bonuses complicate matters in other ways too. Not only do they have the effect of skewing the distribution of rewards between parties to the governance contract, but they can also affect the way in which the company operates.

'The controlling mind' problem

In 2019 it emerged that several Scandinavian banks – among them Swedbank and Danske Bank – had built up large operations in the Baltic states with the express purpose of laundering money for Russian clients (the assumption being that the funds were the proceeds of criminal activity).

It is inconceivable that a diligent board of directors, assisted by proper internal audit, would not have identified the problems. It must be assumed consequently that these companies were deliberately running part of their operations as illegal activities, although the companies passed the problems off as the actions of rogue employees. But if that was the case, who should have been punished by the regulators? The shareholders had delegated the running of the company to the directors; the shareholders would not have known of the details of every operation. The employees and managers (some, at least) were supposedly doing as they were told, although that is often a flimsy excuse, by other senior directors; 'the company' is a vehicle and has no shame. Of the senior directors, how many knew about it?

The corporate managerial emphasis now placed on 'image', fostered by the shallow precepts of 'corporate citizenship', means that companies and their managers are often prepared to dissemble about matters that are now considered to be reputationally significant (in order to maintain a 'clean image') that they would have owned up to a few years earlier. As the scope of public interest has expanded, so has the number of potential transgressions. Yet regulators are always at a disadvantage in finding out about illegitimate behaviour since they are reactive rather than pro-active in their activities. Sometimes this leads to outright criminality.

Outright criminality

In the same year as the Nordic banks were found out, the water industry regulator in the UK (OfWat) fined the holding company of Southern Water,

Greensands Holdings, the huge sum of £250 million for sustained manipulation of the water quality statistics it is required by law to collect.

It later transpired that not only had the company been investigated, but that certain employees of the company had been found guilty of obstructing the regulator, and that they had claimed they were compelled to do so because they had been following the instructions of the 'company solicitor'.

In the summer of 2019, Danske Bank was reported to the police in Denmark for mis-selling products it knew to be faulty. (This is regarded as a fraudulent matter in Denmark, and the police have powers to investigate.) In the past decade the UK banks have had to pay back to customers in excess of £44 billion, which they took in exchange for largely worthless 'insurance' policies to protect credit card debts incurred by their customers. The terms of the insurance were usually rigged with exclusion clauses to ensure that payouts would be impossible. This amounts to a deliberate deception on a breathtaking scale. There is little doubt that these matters are openly fraudulent, that the companies were behaving in a criminal fashion and that they were conducting operations in breach of the law.

Lives have occasionally been lost because of the desire to maintain company profits. In the USA, the aircraft manufacturer Boeing allegedly cut corners to save costs – with the full understanding of senior managers – on certification of flight software on a new aircraft model, the 737 Max. Certain components were eliminated from the flight software systems and manuals, and instructions for pilots were never issued. Three hundred and forty-six people died in resultant crashes. The company has admitted partial responsibility. (In the 1970s, Ford was prosecuted over cost-related failings in the fuel supply design of their Pinto car – an explicit earlier example of corporate disregard of safety when faced with profit gains.)

These instances of course also affect other companies that supply components or services to the companies involved, so there is a huge knock-on effect.

Other actors – the stakeholders

The Cadbury definition is fairly plain in admitting only three groups to any involvement in governance – shareholders, managers and auditors.

Not long after the report was published, a reaction to this limitation was expressed by theorists and activist shareholders who suggested that many other groups should be involved in determining the governance structure, since these other groups had a stake in the future of most companies. The term 'stakeholder' was admitted to the vocabulary of governance, although there is no strict definition of who the stakeholders are. An operational definition is not difficult to devise, but its scope is less certain.

Stakeholders are essentially those who have some interest in the fortunes of the business – that interest may or may not be capable of being expressed in financial or value terms.

Most people would agree that the employees have an interest in the well-being of the companies that they work for, but their interest might not always coincide with those of the shareholders, of course. They want higher wages for their labour. All other things being equal, this will reduce profits – not a desirable outcome for shareholders, since the level of profit is a determinant of the level of dividends.

Customers also want to see the companies they trade with prosper – as do suppliers, creditors and possibly debtors, too. The State has an interest – healthy companies produce healthy tax revenues; well-run companies that do not jeopardise their workers' health or safety reduce the burden on the State to look after people. Insurers don't want to see badly run companies. Residents and adjoining landowners want their commercial and industrial neighbours to run their businesses cleanly without noise or pollution. Some might even extend the list to future generations who will want sustainable resources to help provide for them.

The problem with all these categories of people or organisations who have an interest is one of ranking them in precedence. Who is to take priority? Are shareholders the most important? What about the workers who may have only the company as their source of income? Are the claims of creditors to be settled before those of shareholders?

The law already provides answers to some of these (creditors generally take precedence over shareholders, for instance). But for other issues, the problem is more complicated – mostly because the method of accounting for company profits was devised solely for the purposes of shareholders, well before anyone even considered the possibility of claims by any other parties.

The profit and loss statement, the balance sheet and the source and uses of funds (whatever their current fashionable name) are primarily to allow shareholders to check on the progress of their companies. Methods of accounting that are not focussed on this are called 'social accounting' or 'triple bottom line' accounts. They were first suggested in 1994 by British management consultant John Elkington, who wrote a book (*Cannibals with Forks*; Capstone 1999) which suggested that instead of just profit, company accounts should have two other 'bottom lines' – 'people' and 'planet' – hence the triple bottom line. The format of the accounts is adjusted to produce a result that purports to show the impact of company activity on each of the other subjects. The problem is that the information used for each new category is just a re-ordering of existing information, so such accounts are often criticised as being neither innovative nor accurate.

Corporate social responsibility – are companies 'citizens'?

One of the ideas that solidified from the stakeholder discussion is that companies should have some form of responsibility beyond that of simply producing profits.

The underlying controversy about the purposes of companies had been around for a long time, though. As far back as 1882, the railway mogul W H Vanderbilt had attracted controversy by (supposedly) exclaiming to a newspaper reporter "The Public be damned! I'm working for my shareholders!" (there are many variants of the story, some of which put Vanderbilt's words in a better light).

Slightly less than one hundred years later, the Chicago economist Milton Friedman had declared flatly that a company doing anything other than working for the maximum profit was "flat-out socialism". Two years after that, in 1974, the trustees of the Phillips-Van Heusen Shirt Co pension fund sold their shares in the American company International Telephone and Telegraph at a heavy loss (which may have breached their obligations as trustees) because they objected to what they regarded as the company's anti-social actions in Chile (the company had been implicated in the overthrow of the legitimate government in a military coup).

In the late 1990s the argument took a further turn when activists and academics began to talk and write about extending the concept of corporate social responsibility into one of endowing companies with 'corporate citizenship'. This phrase presumably arose from a view that as companies had 'a part to play' in society, and if they were 'persons' with rights, then they should be commensurately accorded certain obligations to match. It became the fashionable thing for companies to boast about – just before it collapsed in 2007, Lehman Brothers' annual report extolled its virtues as an environmentally conscious 'global corporate citizen'.

The matching of rights and obligations is a valid approach. However, the simple fact is that companies – though they may be legal persons – do not fulfil the requirements of being citizens, partly again because of the issue of the (lack of) corporate mind, which means that they cannot exercise their legal rights in the same way as a human person. Human citizens have the characteristics that they can vote, they can sit in a legislature and they can sit on juries in judgement of their fellows. Companies have no such characteristics and can do none of these things. (Would you really want to have a company involved in voting in elections? Or being involved in passing laws, or deliberating about someone's guilt? Any more than they currently do, of course, through lobbying and corporate propaganda.)

Perhaps because of the realisation of this, the concept of corporate citizenship has largely fallen out of currency since the decade of financial austerity arising from the banking collapse of 2007–2008. Despite its vacuous nature (perhaps because of it), the term is still occasionally met in academic papers.

Lately there has been a resurgence of the controversy about the purpose of companies aside from the generation of profit, with the onset of greater awareness of the climate crisis and the problems of plastic and toxic waste. Renewed debate has ebbed back and forth about the social obligations of companies. Are they there just to make profits for shareholders, or should they take a wider, perhaps environmental, view?

In 2018 the chief executive of the world's largest asset management company, Black Rock, sent out a letter which reminded the boards of other companies that without making a contribution to benefiting consumers and communities (paying proper wages, investing in employees' skills, investing in capital expenditure and innovation) as well as shareholders – *particularly in the face of inaction by governments* – long-term growth would stall. In this view, companies were to be the engines of creating an environment for their own sustainability.

This argument is difficult to refute – the long-term interests of the shareholders are certainly served if the companies are able to sustain their operations. But it still leaves open and unresolved the question of who determines the priorities for social goods – in fact, it seems almost to suggest that such decisions are best left to companies.

At root, all that companies are required to do is to obey the law and pay their taxes. It is best left to real, human persons to decide what those laws might be and what they should cover – a subject which will arise again, in consideration of the governance problems to come, in Chapter 8.

Audit and financial information – what is the value of the audit?

The law in the UK states that all companies must be audited (subject to certain exemptions for 'small' companies), and this is reinforced by the Listing Agreement, which all quoted companies have with the Stock Exchange. Cadbury considered the auditors to be one of the necessary legs of the triangle in establishing good and workable corporate governance.

As the Appendix shows, shareholders might not always agree with him. Given the large number of significant problems that shareholders in public companies have experienced, worldwide, audit might be thought to be the weak link in the governance triangle that Cadbury suggested.

The problem with auditing is a complicated one involving, timing, costs, complexity of information, the availability of staff and the responsiveness of the audited company. For quoted companies in the UK, audits should be completed within the four-month period that is allowed after the end of the company's year for accounts to be produced for shareholders. In large, complicated companies this is a difficult task to achieve without mobilising lots of costly staff, all dependent upon the prompt presentation of information from the host company.

Shareholders rely on auditors to 'prove' the actions of management to them by validating the accounts the managers have prepared. Auditors, however, accept only the obligation to prove for one very specific instant – the moment when the accounts are signed off. The auditors tell the shareholders at this point that the accounts prepared by management give a 'true and fair view' of the state of the company.

They arrive at this conclusion having investigated the accounts – which have been prepared by the directors (or their subordinates) – and it is *the directors* who accept responsibility for the accounts, *not* the auditors. The auditors are merely saying that what the directors have shown them makes sense, is correct *in itself* and does not appear to leave anything out.

The audit is not intended to catch fraud. It may do so as a by-product, but that is not its primary purpose. The problem for both auditors and shareholders is that if management have been purposely misbehaving, then the evidence of deliberate mischief will be hard to find – hence auditors limit their liability to members very particularly and to outsiders even more so (see Caparo v Dickman Industries 1990).

In defence of auditors, it is important in this regard to recognise three things about audits and the audit process:

- Auditing a large and complex organisation is a very difficult task. Auditors will not have the time or resources to investigate every single ledger and every single transaction. They will complete their task on a 'sampling' basis using statistical measures of what they should look for and how deep they should go into the books of the company.
- No organisation always records every transaction perfectly. In consequence the auditors are looking not for complete accuracy but the absence of 'material' differences. In a very large organisation, the value attributed to material can still be very large – even though as a proportion of the totals it will not fall within the limits set by the audit process.

It is for this reason that the accounts have to be signed and dated by a responsible person, the partner in charge of the audit (this obligation was introduced in the Companies Act 2006).

There are a number of reasons why audits have often thrown up problems:

1 They are often used for training new entrants to the accounting profession.

2 There is a pyramidal structure to large audits, with large numbers of junior auditors supervised by a few qualified and experienced staff (who will inevitably take their responsibilities with greater or lesser degrees of care. For instance in 2019, PwC's Leeds office and two of the partners of the firm were fined £6.5 million for repeatedly failing to supervise audits properly).

3 Audits, until recent changes, were often seen as the wedge in the company's door that enabled other more lucrative consultancy services to be sold. Consequently, audits were sometimes priced as 'loss leaders'.

4 Size, volume and complexity pose problems for auditors who always start at a temporal disadvantage in looking at financial information. What they see is *the summary* of lots of transactions – not the transactions themselves.

5 They are dependent upon the information given to them by the directors. For instance, in the summer of 2019, Sports Direct's auditors, Grant Thornton, apparently learnt only at the last minute – just before approving the company's 2019 accounts – that there was a substantial potential tax liability on the company's Belgian subsidiary. This then led to all sorts of problems for Sports Direct in retaining an auditor.

The timing problem of accounting

One of the features of accounting theory is that entries in ledgers have to be *matched* – they have to be placed in chronological, subject and category equivalence when entered into the accounts.

This apparently sensible, straightforward and innocuous requirement can lead to all sorts of problems in the hands of unscrupulous managers who can – in particular – manipulate the timing of events in accounting terms, to flatter profits in some periods and disadvantage them in others. The mechanisms of this are not difficult to follow but are outside the scope of this book. What can be noted, however, is that managers are potentially able to – legitimately – enhance their own rewards through the impact of bonuses that achieve certain targets if they are (collectively) in control of accounting policies, operations and accounting.

Some of these problems will not be flushed out by auditing if the manipulation is sophisticated and neither illegal nor in contravention of accounting principles. This issue is therefore at the nub of the governance problem, and the consequences are very significant.

Managers are potentially able to legitimately and openly massage the effect of commercial operations in such a way that their own rewards are enhanced at the expense of all the other parties to the governance contract – shareholders, employers, customers, suppliers and so on. Furthermore, it is in this area that the Cadbury definition is least able to cope with real-world pressures since the implicit premise of the definition is that individuals will behave in a 'gentlemanly' way towards each other – with rules and principles, honour and good manners – holding sway in the inter-party relationships. As we know, the real world is not like that.

Share marketplace problems – market structural changes; market dynamics; the purpose of the Stock Market

Individually, to repeat, all that shareholders really own is the share certificate detailing the number of shares held. The possession of these may (or may not) entitle them to certain benefits, including the right to receive dividends and the right to vote at annual general meetings (depending on whether the company is a public or private company and in which legal jurisdiction it operates).

Shareholders are heavily circumscribed in how they can to enforce their views. Their rights to make changes are very limited – in particular about the management of the company; how they can censure the directors; what information they receive; how they receive redress; and how they can take action to prevent things they do not like. Larger shareholders may have more leverage either through informal consultation or through combining the power of their holdings in concerted action – but, effectively, not much. This is very different from what traditionalists and most textbooks suggest. As noted previously, small shareholders are excluded from discussions with management where they might voice their views (largely to be fair because they do not have the requisite technical knowledge). Large shareholders often do have such access and are therefore preferred in their influence.

And in a secondary market for shares (which is what all exchanges are) shareholders do not really invest in the companies they buy shares in – they place bets on the performance of the companies, like buying a ticket in a horse race. Even buying shares in 'new issues' often means that the existing owners and promoters of the companies receive the proceeds of the share sales (or at least a portion of them) rather than the companies.

The only 'pure' example of shares being issued by a company to swell its funds is the case of the rights issue where additional funds are raised either for increasing the capital base or reducing the gearing of debt to equity. In all other examples the so-called investment is the exchange of series of obligations on the company to provide information an/or pay dividends.

All this is further complicated by the fact that most small shareholders are even more disadvantaged than individual large shareholders. The structure of modern markets – though a number of provisions are in place to try to make them more equitable – will always favour professional investors who have access to resources which small shareholders do not.

Small shareholders are effectively price-takers in trading shares and have to follow the prices established by large shareholders who can move faster and with better information than small shareholders are able to gather. They do not have access to dedicated trading processes, nor can they expect discounts for trading in significant volumes. Trading is more expensive, less flexible and less easy for small shareholders.

Large 'institutional' shareholders – pension funds, hedge funds and insurance companies – will be privately consulted by the directors of listed companies about a range of options that the company might have to choose from, including managerial pay, dividend policy, strategic developments and so on. When a company chairperson begins an annual statement to a shareholders' meeting by talking about 'their' company, and is addressing a few hundred small shareholders who have come for a day's outing and represent only a few tenths of a per cent of the total number of the company's shares in issue, you know that person is being either excessively polite or excessively patronising (or perhaps, just perhaps, stupid).

Other conceptual problems

Other conceptual problems include:

- unforeseen consequences;
- technological issues;
- concentration of market power;
- letter versus spirit in rule-based and principle-based systems.

The 'law of unintended consequences' has become a popular shorthand explanation of things going wrong (or, very unusually, side effects producing benefits) from a particular action.

It has a long and distinguished pedigree, dating at least from the writings of the seventeenth-century English philosopher John Locke, through to those of the father of economics Adam Smith one hundred years later, to investigations by mid-nineteenth-century mathematicians and most recently to a variant suggested by an American aerospace engineer, Edward Murphy. While working on safety-critical systems for spacecraft, Murphy is supposed to have regularly reminded his colleagues that "whatever can go wrong, will go wrong". The experience is universal: probably some caveman looking at a raging inferno spreading across the savannah grunted the same opinion to his mate after the wind blew a few embers from the campfire. Just like the experience, the application is universal. It applies regularly in matters of corporate governance.

Some economists hold that markets are self-regulating and will allocate resources 'properly' or most efficiently in ways that other systems cannot. However this premise only holds good if certain conditions exist. These conditions include:

- free and immediate flows of costless information;
- no barriers to entry or exit;
- frictionless availability of supply.

A moment's reflection will indicate that these conditions exist nowhere in any market and that markets are therefore only self-regulating under conditions of supervision which bring about some of the preferred conditions. In fact, left to themselves, unregulated markets rarely allocate resources to the most desirable outcome. (The proof of this is very simple. Try to think of a market which is not regulated in some way. It is impossible to do so; even markets which appear to be unregulated at first glance require consistent currency or consistent weights and measures. These have to be regulated by some external agency.) This last effect is particularly the case in stock markets, which free market economists often hold up as paradigms for their case.

In fact, despite the efforts of market regulators, stock markets have a number of flaws, which recent developments in technology have exacerbated further. Not all these need to be examined here, but there are some issues which are significant.

First, not all shareholders are equal. As has already been indicated, given the same piece of information released into the market at the same time, some shareholders can move faster than others, and some are able to use their size to achieve better prices in buying and selling shares.

Second, short-termism (buying and trading on snippets of information rather than a long-term assessment) will produce disturbances in the marketplace that may throw the plans of long-term holders of shares off course. Some types of shareholder (pension fund trustees, for example) are legally obliged to maximise the value of their assets and so may not be able to disregard short-term movements once they reach a certain level.

The introduction of certain super-computer trading systems – including those employing so-called artificial intelligence and algorithmic trading (sometimes called flash-trading or High Frequency Trading) capabilities – have often provoked serious disturbances in the marketplace. On 6 May

2010, $1.7 trillion were temporarily wiped off shares in the New York Stock Exchange when the market entered free-fall after a series of automated trades. Some traders lost and some won during the space of a few minutes that it took for the market to re-establish itself on a stable footing. But in no way can that episode be said to be an effective allocation of resources, nor can it be said that shareholders who might have wished to trade were treated fairly.

One of the characteristics of the automated marketplace is that it now requires huge volumes of trades on tiny margins and with massive churn of stocks to make large amounts of money. Only the very wealthiest and most powerful traders can afford to invest in the equipment needed to extract profit out of such conditions.

In order – again – to try to reduce the anomalies of power between traders, one of the accompanying phenomena to algorithmic trading is the establishing of so-called 'dark pools' where the identity of the traders is protected until after the trade is completed. However, this is itself subject to gaming behaviour ('spoofing' and 'pinging') using the power and speed of super-computers – and pricing in these markets spills over into the more traditional markets used by smaller shareholders.

It has to be recognised that, if the purpose of investing is to make money for the shareholder, a number of different methods of investing have to be made available for those who do not have the desire or the resources to buy shares in a company directly by themselves. They might – for all sorts of reasons, including resources, time, risk aversion, simplicity – want to invest in a collective vehicle where lots of small shareholders' cash is pooled into investing in larger numbers of shares. Collective investment schemes such as this are usually referred to as unit trusts or investment trusts – although the term Exchange Traded Funds (ETFs) has gained popularity recently. The shareholders in these schemes are entitled to the protection of good governance as much as shareholders in companies who have purchased their shares directly. Unfortunately, the record of investment funds is sometimes as murky as that of poorly run companies.

In 2019, it emerged that a 'star' trader in the UK stock market, Neil Woodford, had been investing money from the collective investment schemes that he had run, in companies that were grossly unsuitable for the published requirements that his funds had raised money on. He was running funds supposedly for income (that is, to achieve returns for unit holders by means of a stream of dividends from the companies invested in) when the invested companies were often young start-ups who needed all the cash they generated (and often more) to develop their own markets. The terms of the funds, which were supposed to preclude this, had been subverted by a sleight of hand by Woodford and the negligence of the 'Authorised

Corporate Director' who was supposed to sit on the funds to ensure proper behaviour.

The terms of Woodford's funds required all the companies he invested in to be listed; he invested in companies where the listings were often paper formalities; no trading of the shares ever took place, or even could take place, because they were essentially untradeable. Yet by being 'listed', they satisfied the strict letter of the funds' requirements. As always happens, the subterfuge was discovered when one large investor asked for their money back.

Woodford's deception joins the dishonourable ranks of the likes of Arch Cru and LCF in the UK (see the Appendix) – although it does not match the breathtaking audacity of the Ponzi schemes such as those run by Ivar Kreuger (the 'Swedish Match King') or, in more recent years, by Bernard Madoff.

3   A brief history of corporate governance

Summary

- Corporate governance did *not* begin with the Cadbury Report.
- The early origins of corporate governance.
- The nineteenth century.
- The twentieth century – the development of shareholders' rights through case law and the Royal Mail Line case.
- The reports after Cadbury – carrying on the investigations (mostly): Greenbury; Hampel; Higgs; Turnbull; Myners; the forgotten two – Smith and Tyson.
- The financial crash.
- The post-crash reports – Turner; Walker; Vickers.

Most textbooks – even some from professional institutes – will suggest that 'corporate governance' began with the Cadbury report in 1992. Nothing could be further from the truth. Governance did not spring fully formed in 1992 from the lap of the Cadbury committee. It had a long and complicated history. It was known by a number of names, previously including 'mercantile law', 'contract law', 'company law' and company secretaryship. In its last thirty years it has been concerned particularly with abuses of control and issues of transparency and accountability.

The modern pre-occupation with governance abuses may date from the last decade of the twentieth century, but theorists and legislators have always recognised the need to control corporate appetites. Even as early as 1776, in *The Wealth of Nations*, Adam Smith was very leery of the principle of limited liability. His thinking was that 'negligence and confusion' would always prevail when managers of other people's money did not have the same anxiety over its safety as would be exercised by sole traders and partners. In Smith's view, managers would use the principle of limited liability to escape the debts they incurred through trading.

Among the changes of the late twentieth century that brought about the term, the subject and the concern of 'governance', were:

1   the growing power of the popular press, because of better basic education;
2   the death of paternalistic politics;
3   the importation of American principles of capitalism (which placed greater emphasis, more so than contemporary attitudes in Britain, on making assets work regardless of social implications);
4   the growth of the savings and insurance companies (which produced a 'Wall of Money' that had to be invested).

To these were added the changes demanded of the Stock Exchange by the Thatcher government (itself under pressure from international banks to do so).

The following summary of milestones in the development of corporate governance is not intended as more than a history of highlights and makes no pretension to completeness or comprehensiveness. But it does indicate the rough direction of travel of corporate governance and should dispel the naïve assumption that 'governance' began in 1992.

The earliest manifestations of the corporation occurred in Phoenician times when merchants banded together to fund trading voyages and divided the proceeds according to their contributions to the cost – the original venture capitalists. Records of similar company operations have also been found In Han China (206 BC–220 CE). These ventures would have been regulated by private arrangements, records of which still exist in clay tablets and paper documents.

In the West, the idea of a combination of individuals is derived from the wars of the Middle Ages. Our word 'company' comes from two Latin words that encompass the idea of a band of people breaking bread together. In the Middle Ages, companies of mercenaries roamed Europe willing to fight for the highest-paying State – or wealthy prince who wanted to overturn a State. These companies – of men whose primary attribute was skill at arms rather than learning – used the capabilities of a 'company secretary', whose skills were the reverse of their own, to determine who should receive what from the spoils of the campaigns they fought. Such a man had obviously to be trusted and – if he was to survive – irreproachably honest and fair.

As the small princely wars of the Middle Ages settled into State rivalries, the potential value of commercial activities that were conducted through collective funding were recognised by kings throughout Europe, during the great age of exploration. The right to form corporations to conduct exploration (and exploitation) was regarded as a monopoly of the crown and could be passed on to suitably wealthy purchasers in return for a large amount of money to help fund royal expenditure. It was from grants like this that the great English and European trading companies sprang – among them the Virginia Company (of which John Locke, the English philosopher, was company secretary); the VOC, the Dutch East India Company; Compagnie Française pour le Commerce des Indes Orientales, in France; the East India Company, in the UK (an engine of commerce for 200 years); the Hudson's Bay Company, which still operates in Canada; and, perhaps most notoriously of all, the South Sea Company.

It was this last enterprise which produced the South Sea Bubble – the scandalous speculative frenzy brought about in 1720 by the need to refinance the national debt, achieved through granting a company a monopoly of trading rights with South America. The resulting furore brought about 'The Bubble Act' of 1720 – which prohibited joint stock companies. It was not repealed until 1825. (In the meantime, the unwieldy and cumbersome 'unincorporated association' was the vehicle for collective commercial ventures.) The prohibition on creating private 'joint stock' companies also removed a source of income to the Exchequer and helped paved the way later for taxes on income and capital.

The concept of limited liability, though, was recognised by others outside Britain as a valuable creation. The first limited liability laws were passed in New York in 1811, but because the Americans had not suffered the pangs of the Bubble directly, it still required an act of legislation to create a company.

The legal characteristics of limited liability were then rapidly developed by France and Germany, particularly after the enactment of the 1855 Limited Liability Act in Britain. This came ten years after the Joint Stock Companies Act, which once more permitted companies to be created. In the USA the development of the railways, and the oil and steel industries required by a growing economy, was the driving force behind economic expansion. The statutory requirement of incorporation produced too many restraints for impatient businessmen, and many large businesses dispensed with incorporation as a vehicle and operated as trusts. (The expansion of the railway also brought about developments in accounting – and particularly the styles, practices and conventions of British accounting.)

The Joint Stock Companies Act of 1856 in Britain provided the foundations of modern company law by stipulating a registration procedure for companies which allowed a minimum of seven people to combine their interests into a company.

In 1862 the first Companies Act was passed in the UK, establishing the still-existing pattern of company structure. But in the UK, the law protecting shareholders and distinguishing the company's interests was developed piecemeal through the rules propagated in case law – judge-made law.

Legal rulings established in specific cases provided general guidelines for behaviour: Foss v Harbottle 1843 contributed to the concept that the company has a legal personality; Salomon v A Salomon & Co Ltd 1896 (universally known as Salomon v Salomon) identified the concept of the veil of incorporation; Daimler Co Ltd v Continental Tyre and Rubber Co (GB) Ltd 1916 again dealt with 'the veil'; Gruban v Booth 1917 dealt with oppression of minorities and fraud.

One of the most significant cases in the development of the modern concept of company behaviour was the 'Royal Mail Line case' of 1932 – R v Kylsant and Others. The precise – and fascinating – details of this case can easily be found from numerous sources, but it is sufficient here to note that contemporary accounting practice allowed companies to effectively pay dividends out of 'tax adjustment reserve' accounts and to pad their revenue accounts to produce the illusion of profits – *all completely in accordance with the contemporary rules of accounting*. Furthermore, in the Royal Mail Line case, the court held that there was nothing wrong in this – expert witnesses testified for both the prosecution and the defence – and the case was decided with Lord Kylsant being found guilty not on the matter of the concealment, but of issuing a false prospectus which had concealed the losses his company had incurred for several years, and thereby taking public money under false pretences.

It was not until the Companies Act of 1947 that this sleight of hand accounting was cleared up, and companies were prohibited from operating accounts which they could bolster in good years to feed into the revenue account in lean years. (However, the practice has not died out entirely, and it is still possible to 'legitimately' gently massage the accounts without too much trouble.)

The 1947 Act was rapidly superseded by the 1948 Act of the same name, which gave shareholders the power to remove directors as one of its major reforms. From then on, reforms proceeded piecemeal with only minor and technical changes being made in legislation. All the while, however, case law continued to develop and refine the cross-relationships between the company, the shareholders, the directors and the auditors (see, for instance, Bushell v Faith 1970; Stonegate Securities Ltd v Gregory 1980; Caparo Industries Ltd v Dickman 1990).

In 1986, a sea change took place in the environment in which listed companies operated and their shares were bought and sold. The old relationships that existed between clients, stock-jobbers and stock-brokers were demolished by the 'Big Bang' – the journalistic phrase given to the shake-up in the rules of the City of London's stock exchange. The agreement to change the structure of the market – agreed informally by the Stock Exchange (under pressure) with the government – paved the way for very substantial changes in the operation of markets. It also brought about, simultaneously, significant alterations in the relationships between companies, shareholders, directors and auditors.

These changes soon began to manifest themselves in scandals – the operation of corrupt companies such as Polly Peck and BCCI; misuse of company funds by powerful individuals, as in the Mirror Group pension fund thefts; misbehaviour by stockbrokers, as in the 'Blue Arrow' case; and the wave of salary scandals after nationalised industry privatisations – when previous company functionaries suddenly began to see themselves as 'world-class' businessmen.

These began to be irksome to the public. In the hands-off politics of the times, they were dealt with in a series of reports and committee investigations beginning with the 1992 Cadbury Committee. It was not until fourteen years later, though, that the overall structure of the listed company was finally addressed in the 2006 Companies Act – which might better be called the 2006–2010 Companies Act, since many of its effective provisions were delayed in operation over a period of four years because of the complexity of the changes demanded.

In the period after Cadbury's report, it became immediately apparent that though that committee had blazed a trail, it had done little more than touch on many of the issues which were causing such deep disquiet. For a period of roughly a decade a report on some aspect of governance was issued at about three-year intervals. These reports are dealt with briefly in this chapter. Their major recommendations and findings were consolidated in the Corporate Governance Code of the London Stock Exchange which was first issued in 2000 and has been regularly updated subsequently under the auspices of the Financial Reporting Council (see Chapter 4).

The Cadbury Committee was the first of the committees to consider the relationships between the parties to the operation of companies. It has been dealt with previously. Immediately after it concluded its investigations, it was evident that its report was not a culmination but a threshold that had been crossed, since the report dealt with many issues that required further elaboration if more problems in company behaviour were to be nipped in the bud.

1995

Three years after Cadbury, the *Greenbury Report* was published. Like the Cadbury Report before it, the Greenbury Report was not an 'official' investigation. It was set up by the CBI to investigate the apparent runaway trend of executives awarding themselves higher and higher salaries while shareholders' returns stagnated. In particular the activities of the managing director of the newly privatised British Gas, Cedric Brown, aroused great indignation (and questions in Parliament) when it was disclosed that his salary and pension were rising far above the rate of growth of profits of the company – or returns to shareholders. (Brown had been with BG for forty-four years but suddenly discovered he was a 'world-class executive' the day after the privatisation, while looking in the mirror.)

The remit for the committee was based on identifying (current) best practice in directors' remuneration and preparing a code on that for PLCs to operate by. In other words, the intention was to preserve (at least) the existing arrangements and not consider what might, could or should be done.

One of the prime conclusions of the Cadbury report had been that, to avoid too much self-interest and provide a check on over-vaulting pecuniary ambition, the roles of chairman and chief executive (the term was coming into vogue) should not be vested in the same person. Sir Richard Greenbury, at the time of the preparation of his report, was both chairman and chief executive of Marks and Spencer – having worked there for forty-five years. M&S was then one of the handful of most respected British companies and a foundation stone of the FTSE 100 index. In placing him at the head of the next report, it would be difficult to think of a more blatant establishment snub to the Cadbury recommendations.

The report strove to establish a link between directors' salaries and the performance of their companies and to align the interest of the managers with those of the shareholders. This was to be achieved by splitting directors' salaries into three parts – a basic salary; performance-related pay; and a bonus payable on exceptional performance. It also recommended that a separate remuneration committee should be set up by the board to determine pay outside the normal company decision-making structure. It recommended that this committee should report to shareholders annually – but that shareholders *should not be able to vote on its recommendations*.

The purpose of the remuneration committee was also to set salary packages that would attract, retain and motivate directors of the appropriate calibre – but companies *should try to avoid* paying more than is necessary to do this.

1998

The *Hampel Committee* reported in 1998. Cadbury in his report suggested that the task of developing effective corporate governance was a continuing one. In 1995, the Financial Reporting Council established a committee to review the progress made since the Cadbury report under the chairmanship of the then chairman of ICI, Sir Ronald Hampel. The terms of the committee's remit made no mention of stakeholders' involvement (although it had now become a live topic) and the committee was enjoined always to remember the regulatory burden corporate governance placed on companies.

Unsurprisingly, the report that was produced was very backward-looking – and was roundly criticised for a waste of three years' work in producing little more than a catechism of "no more work required".

1999

The response to the Hampel Report was so deservedly and universally negative that it was probably a relief that only a further year elapsed before the *Turnbull Committee Report* appeared and took the heat off.

Again supported by the FRC and this time led by the finance director of the Rank Group, this committee had been established to review the events surrounding the disastrous lack of internal control which led to the collapse of Barings Bank. It used the work done by the Treadway Commission in the USA to reinforce the argument for transparency of information and effective internal controls and dealt four-square with the duties that auditors had to shareholders, by emphasising the obligations of directors to report to shareholders on regular reviews of operational systems integrity which could then be followed up by auditors.

2001

Two years later, the government of the day finally got around to sponsoring a committee to look at governance under Paul Myners, a senior fund manager (the *Myners Review*) – this time to review institutional investment in the UK. It recommended the adoption by institutional funds of a 'comply or explain' code which would codify best practice in decision-making about investments. It formed the basis of a later Stewardship Code which was produced after the collapse of the financial system in 2007–2008 by Sir David Walker (see later in this chapter).

2003

The final report in the sequence of committee investigations was the *Higgs Report*. It was a return to the mainstream pursuit of governance after the aberration of the Hampel Committee, which so badly misjudged the public mood.

Following the scandals of the collapse of Enron in the USA and Parmalat in Italy, the Higgs Committee looked at the role of non-executive directors. Higgs was part of a trio of three reports – Higgs, Tyson and Smith – and is the only one which really achieved recognition. The conclusions Higgs reached – that there should be at least a numerical balance between executives and non-executives – might or might not have staved off the collapse of either Enron or Parmalat. It is certainly not clear that a numerical balance would have had any benefit in the Enron case, where some supposedly very bright brains were employed as non-executives; and in the case of Parmalat, where there was outright fraud, non-executives would probably also have been of little help.

Tyson (2003) and *Smith* (2003) are the forgotten reports. Neither report made much impact. Dame Laura Tyson of the London Business School looked at the recruitment and development of non-executive directors; the Smith Report dealt with the relationship between a company and its external auditors after the collapse of Enron destroyed Arthur Andersen, seeking to determine general rules and taking its cue from the EU.

After that, everyone took a break from investigating and making reports while they watched the progress of the implementation of the Companies Act 2006 (dealt with in the next chapter) – and then stared fixedly at the financial system while it collapsed.

The crash 2007–2008 and aftermath

The crash appeared to come as something as a surprise to the financial authorities. This was despite the fact that the mistakes, errors and omissions that contributed to the financial panic and crash of 2007–2008 had nearly all been identified in the previous decade's reports on governance in the UK (and the USA's Treadway Commission Report). 'Light touch regulation' which mostly cajoled; 'comply or explain' regimes which achieved neither; 'best practice' which merely pickled and preserved existing problems; and the mantras of 'chasing alpha' and 'increasing shareholder value' which led to headlong pursuit of profit at any risk, all contributed to the crash.

The responses of the authorities in the UK were very mixed. While three reports were commissioned – the 2009 *Turner Review* of the FSA (as it then was) by the then Chancellor of the Exchequer; the *Walker Review*, published in the same year (2009), again sponsored by the Exchequer, which looked at corporate governance generally; and the 2013 *Vickers Commission* which looked specifically at the banks – the *Bank of England* (which arguably should have borne much of the blame for inadequate control) refused to conduct a review of itself until several years later and then did not make the review public.

The conclusions of the other three were also mixed: the Turner Review suggested changes to its operations that should be made in overall 'umbrella' regulation – which partly led to the shake-up of the FSA into three independent components: the Prudential Regulation Authority, the Financial

Conduct Authority and the Financial Policy Committee (inside the Bank of England). The Walker Report came to the laughable conclusion that the corporate governance regime of UK listed companies was 'fit for purpose'; and the Vickers Commission said that the British banks could have six years to fix their problems. In other words, there would be sufficient time for at least one more good crisis before anything changed. As it happened, and completely predictably, the major banks did very little about completing the Vickers requirements (of ring-fencing) until a few months before the deadline.

This Vickers report led to the rush of banks to try to close off their PPI mis-selling obligations in 2019 (later extended to 2020) – a piece of commercial misbehaviour that cost them collectively over £50 billion.

By far the largest single change in the two decades after Cadbury though was the *Companies Act 2006* – a mammoth piece of legislation that was the largest ever passed, in wordage and poundage and time taken to review and implement, by the British Parliament. It formed one leg of a suite of legislation that would effectively provide a platform for detailed regulation by financial and criminal authorities – should they both wish and be able to operate it effectively. It brought about significant changes to the structure of companies and their operations and administration and was supposed to last for a generation.

2019

Since the financial collapse attention has turned to the role of auditors in acting as corporate governance safeguards. The large number of very significant corporate collapses in the last three decades led to calls for the relationship between auditors, companies and shareholders to be reviewed.

The Brydon Review, which reported at the end of 2019, produced an extensive list of suggestions, perhaps signifying how out of touch auditing had become. Among them were:

- a redefinition of audit and its purpose;
- the introduction of 'suspicion' into the qualities of auditing;
- the extension of the concept of auditing to areas beyond financial statements;
- mechanisms to encourage greater engagement of shareholders with audit and auditors;
- a change to the language of the opinion given by auditors;
- the introduction of a corporate Audit and Assurance Policy, a Resilience Statement and a Public Interest Statement;
- greater clarity around the role of the audit committee;

- a package of measures around fraud detection and prevention;
- obligations to acknowledge external signals of concern.

A review released at the same time by Sir John Kingman very severely criticised the UK Financial Reporting Council.

4 The current position of corporate governance in the UK: Part 1

Overall position

- The major pieces of legislation currently controlling companies' activities.
- The Companies Act 2006 – particularly sections 172–176 and their impact on directors.
- The Bribery Act 2010 – wide-ranging but blunt.
- Corporate Manslaughter and Corporate Homicide Act 2007 – an attempt to deal with the 'controlling mind' problem.
- The Criminal Finances Act 2017 – closing the ring on individuals but also against companies.
- Companies Miscellaneous Reporting Provisions 2018 – more significant than its name suggests.
- Financial Services and Markets Act 2000.
- The Listing Rules – the Stock Exchange Contract; premium and standard listing.
- Other rules and regulations.
- ARGA (FCA) accounting standards.

Now that we have looked at the development of corporate governance – and its rapid acceleration in the last part of the last century – this chapter reviews the 'landscape' of governance now existing in the UK. This covers the controlling legislation, the regulations and recommendations. The next chapter examines how issues of governance embodied in these affect the individual parties to company affairs.

It is convenient to divide the major features of current corporate governance into three areas – legislation; significant regulation; and other regulation of note. The following list is not exhaustive of the entire web of governance rules as the list constantly updates – and the trend towards more interventionist action by professional investors is likely to bring more rules rather than fewer.

Legislation

The Companies Act 2006

This is the major piece of controlling legislation which details, among other things, how companies are to be set up; what they require in structure; what they can and cannot do; how public and private companies are distinguished in terms of their structure and administration; the powers, duties and obligations of directors. The Act took four years to fully implement and was the first major overhaul to have occurred in over fifty years, since the 1948 Act of the same name.

In a summary, it is not possible to do more than outline the major features of the Act. Some of these will be dealt with in more detail in the next chapter. Essentially there were five major developments brought about as much of the rest of the wording is just consolidation of legislation (or updating) that was brought into play after the 1948 Act. This accounts for the bulk of the Act.

The main aspects of the Act include:

* a simplified route for company formation (including the abolition of the Memorandum) and new model articles, which companies may use if they have no specific provisions of their own;
* simplified meeting and resolution processes;
* a shortening of filing deadlines for annual accounts;
* a new and simpler method for private companies to reduce their share capital;
* the codification of directors' duties to be set out in a statutory statement;
* provisions to allow greater use of e-communications;
* an introduction of limitation for auditors' liability;
* modestly increased rights for shareholders, through the derivative action process.

Major provisions:

From the point of view of effective corporate governance, the single most significant (though not most important) effect of the Companies Act 2006 was to abolish the requirement that companies must have a qualified company secretary. Prior to 2006 the company secretary was the only company officer that the law required. That person had to be qualified by examination or by experience. After that date, although the functions of company secretary still have to be carried out, no one person is necessarily held responsible for doing so.

The apparently contradictory nature of this requirement is best understood if the Act is seen as being a review of the law relating to small and medium-size companies, for which it was felt that the obligation to have a company secretary was burdensome. The fact that duties still have to be carried out seems, though, to pull the rug out from under this objective. What it did do, however, was allow accountants and lawyers to stand as company secretaries instead, in large companies.

The second major effect was that the Act abolished the requirement for private companies to hold annual general meetings. It was felt that this obligation was being honoured more in the breach than the observation. The Act does *not* say that AGMs *cannot* be held if wished – they can still be requisitioned by shareholders under established rules. It just says that they are no longer obligatory.

The third major change was that the Act established obligations for directors beyond those of simply following the law according to the requirements laid down by various statutes.

Sections 171 to 177 lay down obligations for directors, which are now very similar to those which trustees must observe.

- S 171 lays down that directors must act within powers granted to them by the articles of association and statutory authority. Acts undertaken outside these are *ultra vires* and are subject to penalty.
- S 172 requires directors to act in such a way as to promote the interest of the company. This is a radical departure, and one open to a variety of conflicting interpretations. Its enforcement is also difficult to envisage in isolation.
- S 173 requires them to exercise independent judgement.
- S 174 admonishes them to exercise reasonable care, diligence and skill in performing their duties – again, something of a minefield.
- S 175 requires them not to act under a conflict of interest.
- S 176 requires them not to accept benefits from third parties.
- S 177 gives them a duty to declare a personal interest in proposed corporate transactions.

Since the post of company secretary had been simultaneously abolished, this now placed a burden on directors which they had not previously had to deal with. The company secretary had been the directors' in-house legal guide. Now they were expected to work things out for themselves – or, of course, employ another expensive professional from outside the company to do it for them. (An accountant, perhaps? Or a lawyer?)

The Act also abolished the requirement for companies to have a Memorandum of Association, stating what the purpose of the act of incorporation was supposed to achieve. Years and years of tinkering by lawyers had produced boiler-plate definitions for these mandatory documents that were valueless as statements of purpose. (However, the new problems of governance springing up may well require this policy to be reviewed – see the final chapter.)

Finally, the Act introduced the concept of derivative actions – allowing shareholders to take actions against directors for what they considered wrongful behaviour. However, the bar was set so high for this that the early fears of directors have proved groundless.

The Bribery Act 2010

Even if companies are run procedurally efficiently – meetings are held; votes are properly arranged and counted; regulations observed – they can still go rogue. Eventually this behaviour will bring them into disrepute, and in the late 1990s and early part of the new century a number of such cases arose – the BAe scandal being the most significant. This particular case impinged on the political area and nearly brought down the government of the time.

This piece of legislation makes it illegal for a company either based in the UK or with operations in the UK – or for a British citizen employed by a foreign company – to offer bribes to secure business.

Major provisions:

- It applies to any business which carries on business in the UK ('business' is an undefined term).
- It applies to any agent of such a business – even though the principal may not have complete knowledge of the agent's activities.
- A 'reasonable belief' that a payment is not unlawful is no defence.
- The claim of local custom is no defence.
- It is 'extra-territorial' in that UK citizens working for foreign companies are also covered.

The effect of the Act is to give the courts powers to shut down transgressing businesses. An 'adequate procedures regime' is the only possible defence if a case is brought against a company. This is supposed to signify that the company took every possible step to prevent bribery inside and outside the company.

Until November 2018, the Serious Fraud Office's record in applying the legislation had been patchy – relaying most only on plea bargains by companies or American-style deferred-prosecution agreements where the companies agree to effective probation and good behaviour. But in that month the SFO secured a conviction of the UK managing director of the subsidiary of a French company, Alstom, which had set up a front company to pay bribes to the relative of a Tunisian politician, for winning a tram contract. A year later the company was fined £15 million. Coincidentally, a few days after this fine was reported, Ericsson paid the US authorities over $1 billion to close an investigation into years of corrupt practices in securing telephone contracts in Djibouti, China, Indonesia, Vietnam and Kuwait. The fine was accompanied by a guilty plea to the US Foreign and Corrupt Practices Act and a deferred prosecution agreement lasting three years.

Corporate Manslaughter and Corporate Homicide Act 2007

The problem of the 'controlling mind' and how to punish businesses that commit wrongs has tested legal thinkers and the courts, as shown in earlier chapters. At the turn of the twentieth/twenty-first centuries, several major transport disasters – the losses of the Herald of Free Enterprise car ferry outside Zeebrugge and the Marchioness pleasure cruiser on the River Thames; the Hatfield and Paddington rail crashes; the Kings Cross fire – prompted great public disquiet about the loss of innocent lives as a result of corporate action or negligence. Health and Safety at Work legislation proved unequal to the task of dealing with the problems.

Out of the public and political reaction to these events arose the CMCHA. (The 'Corporate Homicide' clause is necessary since Scots law does not recognise the crime of manslaughter.)

The Act allows an unlimited fine (effective to extinction of the business) if a company is found guilty of causing a person's death by the way that its activities are managed or organised; and amounts to a gross breach of the duty of care owed to the deceased. Companies *and* their directors are both at risk, consequently. In late 2019, a director of a wood chip mill in Cheshire was charged with gross negligence manslaughter over the death of three employees in an explosion, and the company was also charged under the CMCHA. Other managers were charged with HASAWA offences.

Criminal Finances Act 2017

The purpose of this Act is, in the words of the long title:

> to amend the Proceeds of Crime Act 2002; make provision in connection with terrorist property; create corporate offences for cases where a person associated with a body corporate or partnership facilitates the commission by another person of a tax evasion offence; and for connected purposes.

In short, it closes the loop in governance by trying to make sure that companies cannot benefit from the consequences of rogue or illegal behaviour. The Proceeds of Crime Act applies to individuals and not to companies.

Companies (miscellaneous reporting) regulations 2018

This statutory instrument (SI) is far more important than its bland name suggests. To quote the government's own explanatory document:

- Large companies are required to include a statement as part of their strategic report describing how the directors have had regard to the matters in section 172(1)(a) to (f) of the Companies Act 2006.
- Companies with more than 250 UK employees are required to include a statement as part of their directors' report summarising how the directors have engaged with employees, how they have had regard to employee interests and the effect of that regard, including on the principal decisions taken by the company in the financial year.
- Large companies are required to include a statement as part of their directors' report summarising how the directors have had regard to the need to foster the company's business relationships with suppliers, customers and others, and the effect of that regard, including on the principal decisions taken by the company during the financial year.
- Very large private and public unlisted companies are required to include a statement as part of their directors' report stating which corporate governance code, if any, has been applied and how. If the company has departed from any aspect of the code it must set out the respects in which it did so, and the reasons. If the company has not applied any corporate governance code, the statement must explain why that is the case and what arrangements for corporate governance were applied.
- Quoted companies with more than 250 UK employees are required to publish, as part of their directors' remuneration report, the ratio of their CEO's total remuneration to the median (50th), 25th and 75th percentile full-time equivalent remuneration of their UK employees. Alongside this, companies have to publish supporting information, including the reasons for changes to the ratios from year to year and, in the case of the median ratio, whether, and if so how, the company believes this ratio is consistent with the company's wider policies on employee pay, reward and progression.
- All quoted companies are required to illustrate, in the directors' remuneration policy within their directors' remuneration report, the effect of future share price increases on executive pay outcomes. Companies are also required to include a summary in their directors'

remuneration report of any discretion that has been exercised on executive remuneration outcomes reported that year in respect of share price appreciation or depreciation during the relevant performance periods.

The new requirements came into play for company reporting on financial years starting on or after 1 January 2019. The one exception is the requirement for companies to illustrate the impact of share price increases on executive pay outcomes based on any new remuneration policies introduced by companies on or after 1 January 2019.

This obviously begins to put some force behind the issues of pay gaps between employees and directors. However, it merely requires information to be supplied, but interestingly, it places that requirement on very large private companies as well as those whose shares are listed.

Collectively the four laws and the SI form a substantial web of statute that should control corporate governance. But a number of soft spots remain:

- The system of governance is not statutory except for the bare minimum; the principle of 'comply or explain' holds for most governance issues, although gradually the centre of gravity could be said to be shifting towards enforceable rules.
- The courts still have difficulty with the legislation: the first prosecution under the Bribery Act was of a civil servant who took a bribe over an election issue and could as easily have been pursued under existing legislation. Although it must also be recognised that in some ways of course *an absence of prosecution* can be seen as vindication of the legislation.
- The CMCHA still poses problems – the standard of proof required is at a criminal level, not the balance of probabilities test of the civil case.
- The Criminal Finances Act of 2017 has been used successfully to pursue international money laundering through the use of Unexplained Wealth Orders. But the rapid growth of limited liability partnerships (LLPs) which are not required to disclose information in the same way as companies (and are now often the legal form of choice for those who wish to remain at least partially hidden from the law) has made the thicket of detail much denser to investigate.

Financial Services and Markets Act 2000 and amending legislation

While the legislation detailed thus far impacted on companies directly, at the root of much of the structure of corporate governance is the piece of legislation that introduced the superstructure of market regulation – the Financial Services and Markets Act 2000.

This Act brought together a regulatory superstructure for finance markets – and set out the way that 'regulated' companies would have to behave. It put into place a mechanism for the operation of the European directives with which UK finance market operations would have to harmonise. It established the Financial Services Authority as the UK Listing Authority, the body with whose regulations listed companies would have to comply.

The FSMA 2000 was substantially amended by the *Financial Services and Markets Act 2012* when the FSA was replaced by the Financial Conduct Authority (largely as a result of the perceived failure of the FSA during the financial crisis four years earlier) and the Prudential Regulation Authority; and with the creation of the Financial Policy Committee of the Bank of England.

In 2016 the *Bank of England and Financial Services Act* made reforms to the governance of the Bank of England and reforms relating to the financial services sector generally. Among other things, it ended the status of the PRA as a subsidiary of the Bank and established a Prudential Regulation Committee (PRC) in the BoE to exercise the functions of the PRA.

The Act made amendments to the senior managers and certification regime for companies which give any form of financial advice or perform deal execution. The Act also gives the FCA powers to investigate and prosecute insider dealing and market abuse.

Significant regulation

UK Corporate Governance Code

The latest iteration in the code – formerly known as the Combined Code (because it combined Cadbury with the subsequent, major recommendations from those that followed) – dates from 2018 and came into effect on 1 January 2019.

Its major provisions can be summarised as follows:

- According to the FRC (its sponsoring organisation), it emphasises the need for positive relationships between companies, shareholders and stakeholders.
- It stresses the importance of a clear purpose and strategy aligned with healthy corporate culture.
- It indicates the significance of high-quality board composition and a focus on diversity.
- It stresses that senior staff remuneration should be proportionate and support long-term success.

Again, according to the FRC, it is designed to "set higher standards of corporate governance to promote transparency and integrity in business; and attract investment in the UK for the long term, benefitting the economy and wider society".

The Code does not set out a rigid set of rules. Instead it offers "flexibility through the application of Principles" and through the use of the 'comply or explain' rubric it seeks to push companies into 'best practice'. According to the FRC's accompanying introduction, "It is the responsibility of boards to use this flexibility wisely and of investors and their advisors to assess differing company approaches thoughtfully". The latest version of the code is considerably reduced in length from its predecessors with so-called Supporting Principles having been removed from the text. There are in addition, fewer absolute provisions.

Companies which want to have their shares listed are obliged to sign up to the provisions of the UK Corporate Governance Code, which then forms part of the 'listing contract', together with other provisions, between the company and the London Stock Exchange.

The Listing Rules

When a company enters its shares into the public market, it does so through a long process of verification of its records, financial history and future prospects by accountants, lawyers and market administrators.

At the root of this process is a document which effectively forms the contract between the company and the market (in the case of the UK, this is the London Stock Exchange). This document comprises the listing rules – the agreement which controls the governance of the company and which it undertakes to uphold.

The Listing Rules are administered by the Financial Conduct Authority. The FCA used to be called additionally 'The UK Listing Authority', but that term is being phased out (by the FCA) in favour of references to the FCA's 'Primary Market Responsibilities'.

The London Stock Exchange had a previous history of self-regulation ('club regulation', as sociologists would call it) and the Listing Rules are based on this experience, with the added complication that under EU rules all listing requirements had to dovetail to allow the 'passporting' of listings between European exchanges. In practice, this meant the UK rules always met and occasionally exceeded the EU requirements ('super-equivalence'). The Listing Requirements embody the most recent iteration of the UK Corporate Governance Code. Companies are expected to comply with provisions in the code on executive pay, on the 'comply or explain' principle of disclosure and with the obligations regarding shareholder protection and the release of information to the market.

There are twenty separate sections with three appendices:

LR 1, Preliminary: All securities

LR 2, Requirements for listing: All securities

LR 3, Listing applications: All securities

LR 4, Listing particulars for professional securities market and certain other securities: All securities

LR 5, Suspending, cancelling and restoring listing: All securities

LR 6, Additional requirements for premium listing (commercial company)

LR 7, Listing principles: Premium listing

LR 8, Sponsors: Premium listing

LR 9, Continuing obligations

LR 10, Significant transactions: Premium listing

LR 11, Related party transactions: Premium listing

LR 12, Dealing in own securities and treasury shares: Premium listing

LR 13, Contents of circulars: Premium listing

LR 14, Standard listing (shares)

LR 15, Closed-ended investment funds: Premium listing

LR 16, Open-ended investment companies: Premium listing

LR 17, Debt and debt-like securities: Standard listing

LR 18, Certificates representing certain securities: Standard listing

LR 19, Securitised derivatives: Standard listing

LR 20, Miscellaneous securities: Standard listing

LR Appendix 1, Relevant definitions

LR Appendix 2, Fees and financial penalty income

LR Appendix 3, List of regulatory information services

There are three grades of listing:

Premium Listing

A Premium Listing is available only to equity shares issued by trading companies and closed and open-ended investment entities. Issuers with a Premium Listing are required to meet the UK's super-equivalent rules which are higher than the EU minimum requirements. A Premium Listing means the company is expected to meet the UK's highest standards of regulation and corporate governance – and as a consequence may enjoy a lower cost of capital through greater transparency and through building investor confidence.

Standard Listing

Standard Listings cover issuance of shares, Global Depositary Receipts (GDRs), debt and securitised derivatives that are required to comply with EU minimum requirements. A Standard Listing allows issuers to access the Main Market by meeting EU harmonised standards only rather than the UK 'super-equivalent' requirements.

Prior to October 2009 when the FCA introduced new rules, only companies incorporated outside the UK were eligible for a Standard Listing. Now Standard listings are open to all companies regardless of domicile.

The High Growth Segment (HGS)

Launched in 2013, listings in HGS are designed to assist mid-sized European and UK companies that require access to capital and a public platform to continue their growth. It is intended for UK and European trading businesses that can demonstrate significant growth in revenues and a longer-term aspiration to join the Premium segment of the Main Market.

Specific eligibility criteria include:

- The company must be incorporated in an EEA state.
- Listing of equity shares only.
- The listing must apply to a revenue-generating business with historic revenue growth of a minimum of 20% (CAGR) over a three-year period.
- There must be a minimum free float of 10% of the issued shares with a value of at least £30 million (majority of the £30 million must be raised at admission).
- A Key Adviser (who must be a UKLA approved Sponsor) must be retained at admission and for specific matters including notifiable transactions.

Since HGS has EU Regulated Market status but sits outside the UK's Listing Regime, HGS companies are subject to the London Stock Exchange's HGS Rulebook and existing Admission and Disclosure Standards. In addition, as a participant in a Regulated Market, the relevant directives (including the Prospectus directive, Transparency directive and the Market Abuse directive) apply.

Disclosure and transparency requirements

Since 2007 all listed companies throughout the EU have been subject to the Transparency directive of the EU which seeks to harmonise the information released by companies into the marketplace for shares. The Disclosure requirements accompany the Market Abuse requirements.

In the UK these are incorporated in the FCA's handbook which is in fact an electronic source constantly updated with new information. The relevant sections include details surrounding the preparation and form of annual and interim trading statements and management reports; disclosure and control of 'inside information'; control of information by persons exercising managerial responsibility and the means by which information is released to the market.

ARGA (FRC) accounting standards

After a succession of scandals over lax accounting – those involving Carillion and Patisserie Valerie in particular – the government announced that the Financial Reporting Council would be replaced during 2019 by the Audit Reporting and Governance Authority. It is not so much a replacement as a transition – a change of name, a change of acronym and a change of top person. Much of what was previously there will remain in place – although a new ethos is promised particularly in respect of the domination of the audit of large companies by the 'Big Four' (KPMG; PwC; Deloitte; Ernst and Young), to which much of the blame over poor practice has been attached.

The FRC standards are the accounting principles which must be used by companies reporting to their shareholders in the UK. They are different from Generally Accepted Accounting Principles, which is the preferred format for US firms, for instance. These are maintained and updated by the Federal Accounting Standards Board (FASB).

The accounting standards are not simply for accountants. The manipulation of the standards – and, yes, it can be done quite easily by a suitably corrupt, competent accountancy policy – can lead to profound distortions in the governance regime.

Other regulations of note

Stewardship rules

In January 2020 the ARGA/FRC implemented a new set of standards which are to be applied to companies – asset managers – which invest money on behalf of their clients in listed companies – pension funds, investment trusts, insurance companies and so on.

According to the ARG/FRC:

> Stewardship is the responsible allocation, management and oversight of capital to create long-term value for clients and beneficiaries leading to sustainable benefits for the economy, the environment and society.

The Code will seek to impose 'comply or explain' standards on such investors and in particular to make conflicts of interest transparent.

According to the FRC Code:

> All Principles are supported by reporting expectations. These indicate the information that organisations should include in their Stewardship Report and will form the basis of assessment of reporting quality.

When applying the Principles, signatories should consider the following, among other issues:

- the effective application of the UK Corporate Governance Code and other governance codes;
- directors' duties, particularly those matters to which they should have regard under section 172 of the Companies Act 2006;
- capital structure, risk, strategy and performance;
- diversity, remuneration and workforce interests;
- audit quality;
- environmental and social issues, including climate change; and
- compliance with covenants and contracts.

While the purpose of the Code is therefore reasonably clear, the benefit of the code is not, since any effective manager would presumably be operating in such a way already. However, if there is a conflict – open or implicit – in the desires of a certain number of clients to vote in a certain way and the asset managers position (which may happen particularly in respect of trustee funds) then it is unclear how the asset managers will resolve the issue. The FCA certainly does not have any teeth with which to impose the Code.

Quoted Companies Alliance rules

While 'comply or explain' is not intended to be prescriptive in detail, it does not necessarily fit the circumstances of all companies. Cadbury stated in the introduction to his original report that he hoped that all companies would incorporate some form of governance procedures broadly in line with his platform.

The QCA is an organisation that represents small and medium quoted companies and in 2018 produced its own revised version of a governance code, which they claim:

> is a practical, outcome-oriented approach to corporate governance that is tailored for small and mid-size companies. It is a valuable reference for growing companies wishing to follow good governance practice.

It includes 10 corporate governance principles that companies should follow, and step-by-step guidance on how to effectively apply these principles.

Again, according to the QCA:

> [The] Code is especially relevant in that London Stock Exchange has changed the AIM rules so that all AIM companies are required to apply a recognised corporate governance code and explain how they do so since September 2018 [*sic*].

Wates Principles

The Governance Code applies only to listed companies. The QCA has sought to modify it through its own set of principles. The Wates Principles apply to those companies (some of which may be very large, of course) which are still private and have no listing. It is, obviously, exhortatory.

Principle one: purpose

An effective board promotes the purpose of a company and ensures that its values, strategy and culture align with that purpose.

Principle two: composition

Effective board composition requires an effective chair and a balance of skills, backgrounds, experience and knowledge, with individual directors having sufficient capacity to make a valuable contribution. The size of a board should be guided by the scale and complexity of the company.

Principle three: responsibilities

A board should have a clear understanding of its accountability and terms of reference. Its policies and procedures should support effective decision-making and independent challenge.

Principle four: opportunity and risk

A board should promote the long-term success of the company by identifying opportunities to create and preserve value and establishing oversight for the identification and mitigation of risks.

Principle five: remuneration

A board should promote executive remuneration structures aligned to the sustainable long-term success of a company, taking into account pay and conditions elsewhere in the company.

Principle six: stakeholders

A board has a responsibility to oversee meaningful engagement with material stakeholders, including the workforce, and have regard to that discussion when taking decisions. The board has a responsibility to foster good stakeholder relationships based on the company's purpose.

The principles are anodyne and barely worth the effort put into them. They could have been drawn up on the back of an envelope in an afternoon. There is little to be disagreed with in any of them. In fact, they might almost be called a statement of the obvious.

5 The current position of corporate governance in the UK: Part 2

Individual provisions

- How the law currently impacts the individual participants in corporate governance.

This chapter refers to the relevant laws on company behaviour as of December 2019 (principally the Companies Act 2006 and supporting legislation). The law on corporate governance will almost certainly change as a result of the UK's departure from the EU in January 2020.

Shareholders

The Companies Act 2006 has no section specifically about shareholders. Shareholders' rights are usually explained by reference to other specific issues contained in sections dealing with:

- the Articles of Association;
- the issue, allotment, registration and disposal of shares;
- the election of directors;
- the appointment of auditors;
- the accounts;
- dividends;
- the general meeting;
- insolvency.

All companies are *limited liability* entities – their shareholders are not at risk for the debts of the company to any greater extent than the shares they hold – unless the limitation of liability is *by guarantee*, in which case they are limited to the extent of their guarantee. (Incorporation with unlimited liability is possible but largely pointless.)

Companies are of two main types: private limited and public limited. Public limited companies may also have their shares listed on exchanges;

private companies may not. Private companies are designated 'ltd' or per-haps 'Ltd' (the style must be consistent), while public limited companies are either 'plc' or 'PLC' (again, the style must be consistently applied). Once a private company reaches a certain size in terms of share capital (£50 000, one quarter of which must be 'paid up'), it may if it wishes re-register as a public limited company. Private limited companies are therefore mostly small entities, and public limited companies (which may or may not be 'listed') are larger.

The protection of shareholders' rights in all companies is effected by means of the Articles of Association. Where no articles are specifically written for a company, then the so-called model articles of the Companies Act 2006 will apply when the company is registered at Companies House. These model articles contain certain minimum provisions which must be applied – registration, registered address, legal name, share register and protections of inspection and maintenance of the register, levels of autho-rised and issued capital and so on.

Registration is mandatory – if there is no registration, then there is no legal company. If there is no registered company, transactions by the entity calling itself a company and by those making the transactions then become illegal and fraudulent.

In private companies, the articles can be whatever the members agree to, provided there is no obvious illegality or contravention of statute. Provided the basic statutory requirements are met and the terms of the articles are observed in transfers of shares, voting rights and procedures and so on, the courts have no basis to interfere in matters of shareholdings. The articles form a contract between shareholders and the company, and courts will not interfere in matters of voluntarily entered contracts unless there is some illegality.

Private companies can also have shares in a variety of forms of share which are not available to public companies whose shares are listed. These can include convertible shares, redeemable shares, preference shares and various combinations of these. It is also possible – but very unusual – for shares to be issued as 'bearer' shares without any name being entered in the share register and possession of the shares signifying entitlement to ownership.

Unlisted UK companies are required to identify persons who exercise sig-nificant control (PSCs), usually through their shareholdings, and to publicly disclose their details in a separate company register (the PSC register). They must also record the particulars of relevant legal entities that would hold significant control if they were individuals. Listed companies meet these obligations through the listing requirements of the UK Stock Exchange.

Private companies are no longer required to have a company secretary nor to hold annual general meetings, although they may have both if they wish. However, the functions for which the company secretary was responsible must still be carried out. It could be argued that the elimination of the obligation to hold an annual general meeting diminishes the position of shareholders. Proponents of the removal would argue no doubt that there is no prohibition of meetings, merely a flexibility of when and if they are held.

In public companies, the position is different. First, the company must have an identified person who acts as company secretary – although increasingly, large companies are adopting the American term 'General Counsel' to identify the person who fills the advisory function of the company secretary in ensuring the actions of the board are legal. This person need not be a chartered company secretary, as was previously the case before the 2006 Act. The company secretary is responsible for the maintenance of the company's share register (and sometimes this function is outsourced to registrars).

Second, the range of shares available to a public limited company whose shares are listed is reduced to ordinary shares – although companies may issue preference shares which have no voting rights. These are entitled to a fixed rate of return but not to vote at annual general meetings or other company meetings.

Third, plcs (or PLCs) must hold annual general meetings to present their accounts and have them approved by the shareholders; to elect and re-elect directors; to approve dividend payments (but not to alter them, except to deny them); and to approve the selection and appointment of auditors. Any meeting that is not an annual general meeting is an Extraordinary meeting.

Ordinary motions (which become resolutions if passed) are put to the shareholders if they only involve matters of ordinary business permitted by the articles. Special motions (again, which become resolutions when passed) go to the heart of the contract between the company and the shareholders – the issue of new shares, or fundamental changes to the company. (In recent years the distinction between motions and resolutions has become blurred.)

One of the most important aspects of shareholders' rights is provisions in statute (and possibly additionally in the articles) which protect their positions in the company's shareholding structure. *Pre-emption rights* allow shareholders to ensure their shareholdings are not diluted as a proportion of the overall shareholding by being offered a proportion of any new issue of shares which matches their existing holding. Minority shareholders' rights vary depending on the percentage of shares they hold in the company.

Shareholders holding 5% of the issued shares may do the following:

- apply to court to prevent the conversion of a public company into a private company;
- call a general meeting;
- require the circulation of a written resolution to shareholders (in private companies);

- require the passing of a resolution at an annual general meeting (AGM) of a public company.

Shareholders with a higher percentage of the issued shares also may do the following:

- With at least 10% of the issued shares, they have the right to call for a poll vote on a resolution.
- With more than 10%, they have the right to prevent a meeting being held on short notice (in private companies).
- With more than 15%, they have the right to apply to the court to cancel a variation of class rights, provided such shareholders did not consent to, or vote in favour of, the variation.
- With more than 25%, they can prevent the passing of a special resolution. (Special resolutions go to the heart of the contract between shareholders and the company.)

In addition, all shareholders, acting on behalf of the company, have the right under the 2006 Companies Act to apply for a *derivative action* against the company's directors (ss 260–263 of the CA 2006) if they believe that the directors' actions have been prejudicial to their position. However, these actions are subject to passage through a number of 'gateways' and the allowable routes to using them are restricted. (Shareholders have always been able to apply for remedies in the event of some form of oppression – in fact, the rules established in Foss v Harbottle 1843 might be said to be the root of minority protections – but the 2006 Act codified and simplified the issue.)

The company secretary

Prior to the passing of the 2006 Companies Act all companies had to have a company secretary. The 1948 Companies Act gave statutory recognition to the company secretary for the first time, and in 1971 the courts recognised the real extent of the company secretary's authority and responsibilities: the company secretary was the *only* officer which all companies were required to have.

This obligation was rescinded by the 2006 legislation, and from 2008 it became the case that only plcs are required to have company secretaries (although all companies still have to discharge the functions that were previously the province of the company secretary). It is increasingly the case that the advisory and registry functions of the company secretary are being split.

The company secretary may not be an undischarged bankrupt or the auditor of the company, but a director may also be company secretary.

The board

The board of directors is the chief agency through which the company is operated. The board is of course composed of individual directors, and it is on these persons – real or legal – that the Companies Act bears, rather than 'the board' itself.

Boards may consist of legal persons, but at least one director must be a real person. Board meetings should be minuted, and those records are private to the company and may not ordinarily be inspected by shareholders.

Boards usually operate on the basis of majority decisions, with the chairman's vote not necessarily being cast to maintain the status quo, in the event of a split decision.

Individual directors

The first issue to note about directors is that they may only act within the powers granted to them by the articles of association. Actions outside these powers are *ultra vires*.

Private companies are not obliged to have a specific number of directors – the law is silent on this point. However, the Companies Act does require that one director be a real person. This provision obviously relates only to private companies since listed companies are required to have real persons as directors.

While companies must indicate who their directors are on their official documents, the personal addresses of those directors are not required to be disclosed.

The impact of ss. 172 to 176 of the Companies Act 2006 has already been dealt with (see Chapter 4). Directors now have a statutory obligation to provide for the long-term interest of the company, although how this duty is to be enforced is debatable. Presumably if there were to be an emissions scandal like that which engulfed Volkswagen a few years back, then shareholders could take action against the directors. As yet, the long-term interest provision has not been tested in the UK courts.

Directors must be elected by shareholders and usually serve for a renewable term of three years. Directors must be at least 16 years of age; however, the upper age limit for directors was abolished by the 2006 Act. Public companies with listings have a more formal appointment regime which has to involve a nominations committee, provided for under the terms of their listing agreements.

Directors are allowed to have nominated *alternates* who can stand in their stead during time of necessary absence or incapacitation. The alternate's appointment is in the gift of the director, not the board – although the board may reject someone regarded as unsuitable. Alternates are entitled to vote at board meetings and may use their discretion in matters of voting.

Occasionally companies may be subject to the influence of persons who are outside the board and who, for a variety of reasons, exercise some control over the company's actions. Such persons are known as *shadow directors* – "a person in accordance with whose directions or instructions the directors of a UK limited company are accustomed to act". While not illegal, the existence of a shadow director contravenes s 173, which requires independent judgement on the part of all directors. In the event of a company failure, shadow directors may be held equally liable for the company's problems, as the named directors.

Where a director may have breached his obligations – perhaps by acting outside his or her powers – shareholders are able to ratify the action after the event through the application of s 239 of the Companies Act 2006. This, if you like, is the flip side of the derivative action provisions, where a director may be pursued for actions that are *ultra vires* and injured the company.

Persons Discharging Managerial Responsibilities (PDMRs) are senior members of the company – those with access to sensitive information – who must be named by the company. They are required to notify the market authorities and the company about every trade they make on their own account in the company's shares within three days. The requirement extends to those 'closely associated' with the individual PDMRs.

The company

The primary piece of legislation to which companies of all sizes are subject is the Companies Act 2006. At its simplest, this requires all companies to have a registered address to which correspondence can be served; requires that one real person be a director; and requires a register of shareholders to be kept (which is available for inspection by shareholders at certain times) and certain other issues regarding its name, which must be in legible lettering, on all the company's business letters, website and emails, on all its notices and other official publications.

In addition, on all its business letters, website, emails and order forms, a company must show in legible lettering:

- its place of registration and its registered number;
- the address of the registered office.

A company does not have to state the directors' names on its business letters but, if it chooses to do so, it must state the names of all its directors. In other words, a company cannot be selective about which directors' names it shows – it must show all of them or none of them.

Under the rule in Foss v Harbottle 1843, if a wrong has been done to a company, then the appropriate remedial action through a claim, should be taken *by the company itself*. The process of derivative actions breaks the logical knot of how this process begins by allowing shareholders either to take the initiative or to ratify directors' actions.

Whether a wrong has been done is usually determined by reference to the Articles, since such cases will usually arise from 'internal' actions. Where wrongs are done by a third party, the remedy and the claim route are usually obvious

Companies which enter into any form of international trade are required under the terms of the Bribery Act 2010 to maintain and demonstrate that they have an anti-bribery regime in place.

Companies with a turnover of £36 million or more are required to maintain an anti-slavery regime under the Modern Slavery Act 2015 to ensure that they and their supply chains have taken action against human trafficking and modern slavery. This, like the Bribery Act provisions, is a matter for the company's board to ensure.

Market obligations

The transition from a company without its share listed to one that is will usually require a number of changes to the corporate governance structures. These new obligations will all be governed by the Listing Agreement.

The most likely structural requirement is for the introduction of a directors' remuneration report and a change in the company's articles to give shareholders the right to vote on this (although the result of the vote is not binding).

Because of the need to allow potential and existing shareholders to take a view on the likely movement of the company's shares, more detailed disclosures will be required in the business review section of the company's annual report than might previously have been included. Since the directors will now be at risk for these statements – given that compliance under the Listing Agreement is the responsibility of the directors – if they are made recklessly or without care, then there has to be additional effort expended to ensure that the comments made are accurate and completely truthful.

To comply with the rules of the FAC (ARGA) handbook under section 7.1 of the Disclosure Guidance and Transparency Rules companies with Premium or Standard listings are required to have an audit committee. At least one member of this committee must be independent of the management and one member must competent in financial matters.

Listed companies are required to explain in their annual reports how they apply the principles of the UK Corporate Governance Code. Specifically they must explain how they comply with its more detailed provisions – or if they do not comply they must explain why not. The provision about the chief executive and the chairman being separate often prompts change.

In this respect in many newly-listing companies, the former owners will retain significant stakes after listing. (In fact one of the things that the Exchange looks for is some form of managerial and ownership continuity.) Any members of management and any directors nominated by key (existing) shareholders will not be considered independent in terms of the Code's standard provision that at least half the board should comprise independent non-executive directors.

For entry to the junior markets, the London Stock Exchange recognises that the detailed provisions for main market listing may not be appropriate for growing companies and that the main market code is a standard to which junior market should aspire.

Companies entering the Alternative Investment Market (AIM) are allocated Nominated Advisers (NomAds) and it the task of these advisors to guide the company through the development of its governance procedures (among other things). If the NomAd resigns, the listing of the company is suspended.

Market abuse

Companies must ensure that members of their own staff and directors observe the so-called closed periods when trading in shares is not allowed because of the likelihood that information may be held by directors and staff that is sufficiently important about forthcoming results.

Companies may only release information to the market through the Exchange's Regulated News Service.

Reporting

Listed companies must provide shareholders with annual and half-yearly financial reports, which have to be released through the market's own news service.

Annual reports must be produced within four months of the financial year end and half-yearly reports within two months of the end of the first six month period of the financial year.

Annual reports must contain a detailed business review. Interim reports must describe important events in the half-year. Both annual and interim reports must include a description of the principal risks and uncertainties facing the business.

Shares

The European Transparency Directive provisions on disclosure of major shareholdings are enacted in the UK through the FCA (ARGA) Disclosure and Guidance on Transparency Notes No 5 which replaced similar provisions in the 1985 Companies Act. The principal changes that were made were in respect of thresholds for disclosure and the removal of certain exemptions.

Notifications are required where a person controls the exercise of voting rights attached to shares rather than where a person simply acquires an interest in shares; this would apply where an 'indirect shareholder' who is not a registered shareholder but who controls the exercise of voting rights. In addition, certain contracts such as options, futures and forward rate agreements can give a person the unconditional right to acquire shares to which voting rights are attached or the discretion to acquire them; yet under the old rules these transactions would not have given rise to an obligation to notify.

Disclosure by fund managers and other professional investors are at a threshold initially of 5% and then 10% (and at every 1% threshold above 10%).

A person appointed as a shareholder's proxy and able to exercise voting rights at his discretion in the absence of specific instructions will be an indirect holder of shares. One consequence of this is that proxy forms appointing the chair of a meeting as proxy for shareholders usually entitle the chair to exercise discretion as to how to vote on other business which properly comes before the meeting. Unless proxy forms appointing a chair as proxy limit the power to voting only on adjournments, the chair will have a notification obligation under DTR5.

There is a notification deadline for shareholders of two business days, and the company has an obligation to notify the market by the close of the next business day. Consequently companies must announce, at the end of each month during which there has been a change in its share capital, the total number of votes attributable to issued capital and the amount of that capital.

6 Corporate governance around the world

Particular features

- A selective examination of corporate governance regulations from significant economies.
- Brief histories and background factors affecting the development of governance.
- Major reports and regulations.
- Current issues in governance for each country.

Whole books have been written about the corporate governance regimes and structures of most of the major economies. This chapter will identify the major features of some of the major economies to indicate the variances that affect the application of governance worldwide. A summary is necessarily brief, and more detail can be found on specialist websites, particularly that operated by the European Corporate Governance Network (www.ecgi.global).

The European Union and individual countries: origins

Formed from the European Coal and Steel Community, the original membership was France and Germany (plus Belgium) collaborating over the marketplace for raw materials that had provided the impetus for the First and Second World Wars. Britain, for a whole variety of reasons, stood aloof, despite the intention of the founding members that the UK should participate.

This loose combination gradually developed into an economic union and then potentially a political union, with particular attention paid to civil and market freedoms including the freedom of movement of persons, capital, services and goods, abolition of trade barriers (enhancing market access) and the removal of externalities to trade.

As a necessary corollary, all national company legislation has had to harmonise with EU legislation. This has impacted the UK through the European Court of Justice; the Financial Services and Markets Act 2000, particularly through the Markets in Financial Instruments Directive (MiFID) and its iterations; and the Shareholder Directive, Transparency Directive and Market Abuse Directive. It is fair to say, though, that in many cases all the UK had to do to conform was indicate 'super-equivalence' (that is, superiority) to these provisions because of pre-existing legislation or rules.

Companies with a base in the EU are permitted to adopt a *Societas Europaea* format, which allows them to register as companies under European law and gives them certain protections from the legal regulations of any single European jurisdiction.

One of the unseen developments of European regulation has been in share settlement, where ownership and title and settlement obligations in shares in European companies traded across European stock exchanges have been dealt with by Euroclear. Based in Belgium and originally part of J P Morgan, the company was set up in 1968 to deal with the settlement of Eurobond deals but has since expanded to deal with all forms of traded instruments.

Italy

The Italian economy is characterised by

- at least seven different types of company structure;
- a low proportion of listed companies;
- heavy state involvement, although this has fluctuated in the past decade;
- heavy family involvement;
- pyramidal cross-holdings between companies which often have strong 'block-holdings';
- a codified civil law – which is not particularly sympathetic to minorities;
- a preponderance of the unitary board structure with a board of auditors that runs alongside;
- capricious tax regimes.

Corporate governance came to Italy slightly later than the UK. The Draghi Report/Law (1998) required the establishment of a board of auditors independent of the directors of the company. In the same year the Preda Report which was named after the chairman of the Borsa Italiano, the Italian Stock Exchange, who sponsored the report. It made comprehensive suggestions concerning the format of governance. In particular, it addressed

- the role of the board – scrutiny of plans, consultation with auditors, establishment of appropriate committees, oversight of remuneration, supervision of general performance;
- the composition of the board;
- the appointment of independent directors;

- the role of the chairman – delegation of powers to the chairman and combination of the two principal roles;
- information required by the board;
- the status of confidential information;
- the remuneration of directors;
- matters of internal control;
- transactions with related parties and conflicts of interest;
- the role of institutional investors;
- shareholder meetings;
- auditor qualifications.

However, Italian business has been plagued by significant scandals. The history of corporate governance (as elsewhere, to be fair) can often be seen as responses to these.

The Parmalat affair

The company was founded in the 1960s by Carlo Tanzi and his chief associate Fausto Tonna. Originally a small pasteurisation plant in Parma, it grew rapidly, taking advantage of de-regulation in the dairy market in Italy and the break-up of the State monopoly. (The regulation of monopolistic tendencies of Parmalat was never pursued by State authorities.) The company was listed on the Milan bourse in 1991. The board was dominated by family or friends of Tanzi, and the family retained control.

The accounts were falsified for over ten years. The company collapsed on Christmas Eve 2003 with debts of €14.3 billion. Expansion had been funded by bonds (which were not as superficially risky as debt for funding banks). The company used similar tactics to Enron (see the section on the USA) in its approach to analysts and banks, bullying them into co-operation on the threat of withdrawing business; higher margins than competitors were never explained; turnover slipped but profits increased.

Grant Thornton – to whom the audit was sub-contracted by Deloitte & Touche – had signed off accounts on the basis of a forged document – which was never independently verified – purporting to show investments in the company's off-shore subsidiary, the Epicurum Fund, matching the debt obligations of the company.

Much of the money that was lost has never been traced. It is almost certain that Parmalat was a laundry business rather than a dairy products company.

The Banco Ambrosiano affair

Based in Milan (Italy's main stock exchange is based there; Milan has the money; Rome has God) the Banco Ambrosiano was closely connected with the Vatican (the Bank's largest single shareholder), the Masonic Lodge P2 (of which Silvio Berlusconi was a member) and the Mafia – for money laundering. (The P2 lodge was also implicated in the bombing of the 1980 Bologna railway station through its 'master', Licio Gelli, during the deep social unrest in Italy in the 1980s and 1990s.)

The bank's managing director, Roberto Calvi, stole money from the Mafia as it passed through the bank – which was supposedly regulated – and the Mafia wanted it back. Calvi fled to London, and the Mafia traced him and killed him but without finding its money.

The Monte dei Paschi affair

In December 2019, thirteen former bankers from the Siennese bank Monte dei Paschi, Nomura and Deutsche Bank were sentenced to jail terms after being found guilty of concealing billions of Euros of losses suffered by the bank between 2008 and 2013 by using complex derivative instruments. The bank, which is the oldest in the world, having been founded in 1472, was nationalised in 2017, after years of being on the brink of collapse and inter-managerial strife brought about by the struggle between major shareholders. The near collapse of the bank and the misuse of funds was major cause of the rise of populism in Italy.

France

Until comparatively recently France had no diverse or well-established investment community: in the late 1990s, only 8% of French households hold shares – compared with about 40% in the USA and 75% in the Netherlands. There was little pension fund involvement in the funding of industry.

The French economy was characterised by

- a powerful family-controlled small business sector;
- strong State involvement in industry;
- a unified educational background of leaders in all sectors – the 'ENArques', so called because of their attendance at the same elite state schools, the ENA;
- 'Dirigisme' – heavy state control of both sectors and individual companies;
- 'Noyaux durs' – crucial holdings of a few large shareholders;
- 'Verouilllage' – revolving doors; senior staff switching between the State and the private sector;
- commercial banks which were often also major shareholders in the companies that they offered clearing services to;

- 'the commanding heights of the economy' which were and to some extent remain State controlled or influenced: aviation, armaments, banks, electronics, engineering, telecoms, oil, pharmaceuticals.

The French idea of corporate governance is also inevitably affected by their legal system. The Code Napoleon specifies and prohibits actions (in comparison with Anglo-Saxon law which, if anything, permits actions not specifically prohibited and encourages development of legal latitude). The French judicial system is investigative rather than accusatory and subject to a centralised administration.

Company characteristics:

- Company structure is divided into two types: SA (Societe Anonyme) – like a plc; or SARL (Societe anonyme a responsibilite limitee) – like a limited company; the Societas Europaea is of course also available.
- Multiple voting rights for certain shares is a feature of some holdings.
- The economy is still heavily dominated by small business units.
- There is a reasonably strong trade association structure and heavy unionisation in larger industries.
- Board structure can be either unitary or dual with limitations.
- Vienot II permits unitary board and separated roles of chairman and chief executive.
- Extremely powerful chief executives: the French chief executive is called the President Directeur-General (PDG) and has responsibility for both day-to-day and strategic direction of the company. The post possesses virtual control of the board through the appointment function.

The legal framework offers generally poor protection to minorities.

As with other European countries, France took its cue from Britain and began to implement reports and changes after the early years of the 1990s.

The first of these was the Vienot report (Vienot I, as it came to be known subsequently). Published in 1995, it was set up by two employers' associations and chaired by the head of Societe Generale. The report established the basic need for reform and concentrated on the role of the board of directors.

Published four years later, Vienot II reinforced the limited impact of the first report and in particular gave companies the right to opt for a unitary board with separated roles of chief executive and chairman. Previously if they wanted this they had to have a supervisory board structure. The alternative was a single board with the functions of CEO and chairman combined.

The Bouton report in 2002 emphasised the importance of specialist committees, defined the role and operation of the board, suggested a format for the composition of the board, dealt with board evaluation and touched on social and environmental issues.

The financial crisis of 2007–2008 was seen by some French commentators largely as a result of the import of Anglo-Saxon business culture, but it is interesting to note that the trigger was the freezing to withdrawals of three investment funds by Banque Paribas when it lost confidence in the underlying assets backing the funds (having been sold to them by American financiers).

Germany

Germany was unified as a nation only at the end of the nineteenth century, and its industrial development was propelled by imperial ambitions in the early twentieth century leading to rivalry with Britain and France. The re-unification of East and West in the 1990s and 2000s brought about retardation in economic growth, although the Germans were seriously affected by the banking crisis – Frankfurt is the second largest European stock market – and has also been affected by its king-pin position in the Eurozone.

As in the UK, there is a centralised body for company registration and de-registration. The *Amtsgerricht-Handelsregister* is the sole government entity for enforcing registration and deregistration of corporate entities.

Governance reform arrived late in Germany – perhaps because of the success of German industry. Germany's equivalent to the Cadbury reforms is the Cromme Code (2002) which was revised in 2010. Under the system put into effect by the Cromme Code, all companies are either GmbH (private with limited liability) or AG ('joint stock' widely held shares). Boards must be two-tier for AGs (the so-called Rhenish system) and may be two-tier for GmbHs.

If employed numbers for GmbHs are below 500 employees, then the company has a managing director (Geschaftsfuhrer) responsible to shareholders. For more than 500 employees, the company must have a supervisory board and a management board. This is required even if the company is owned by one person (real or legal).

The supervisory board (*Aufsichtsrat*) appoints, supervises and may dismiss members of the management board (*Vorstand*). The supervisory board has both members elected by shareholders and members appointed by employees and management – all sets must act in the interests of the company. The supervisory board never has more than two members of management in order to ensure independence from management, and board members may neither hold directorships with nor act as advisors to important competitors of the company

The Aufsichtsrat May be composed of bankers (usually), business experts and other stakeholders and under the 'Insider' system – members of the supervisory board are primary insiders under the Securities Trading Act (*Wertpapierhandelsgesetz*).

The supervisory board approves the distributions of profit and assures itself of the integrity of accounting and financial reporting systems. It meets three to four times a year and produces a written report for shareholders.

The Vorstand is responsible for independently managing the company and is jointly accountable for the enterprise. It performs the function of a British board in that it co-ordinates the strategy of the enterprise, is required to act in the company's interests and undertakes to increase the *sustainable value* of the enterprise. It reports back to the supervisory board on:

- intended business policy and strategy;
- profitability – particularly return on equity;
- state of the business and condition of the company;
- transactions having a material effect on liquidity or profitability.

It also

- prepares motions for submission to the shareholders meeting which are approved by the Aufsichtsrat;
- is responsible for corporate governance implementation – and reports on deviance from the Cromme Code and for the management of internal risk;
- requires its members to accept strict non-compete provisions while occupying board positions.

The 1998 KonTrag (the Law on Control and Transparency in Business) expanded the management board's responsibilities to include formal reporting to the supervisory board on personnel, finance, investment and affirmation that adequate internal monitoring takes place.

The 2000 version of the Cromme Code requires board members to be allocated specific spheres of responsibility for which they have been deemed competent and requires that all operational functions should be represented on the management board. Decisions of the Vorstand are supposed to be unanimous; in the event that agreement cannot be reached, a twenty-four-hour period is to pass before a majority decision can be accepted. Although the chairman can over-rule a majority decision, that decision is subject to review at the next management board meeting.

For the larger AG companies, the provisions are as follows:

- The Vorstand is responsible for both management and strategic issues.
- AGs must have an *Arbeitsdirecktor* responsible for personnel matters.
- The board is usually elected for five years.

- The supervisory board must have at least twenty members who are elected by shareholders and employees.
- For companies of between 500 and 2000 employees, two-thirds of the board members are from shareholders and one-third are from employees.
- Above 2000 employees, the proportions are equal.
- All board members are obliged to act in the interests of the company.
- Supervisory board members may be selected from retiring management board members.

Committee structure:

- usually chairman and vice-chairman, plus two or three others;
- business committee;
- personnel committee;
- investment and finance;
- audit;
- corporate governance.

Until recently, federal tax structures and a lack of incentive schemes made remuneration committees largely unnecessary. However, this has changed in recent years with increasing levels of executive pay.

The USA

The American variant of 'financial' capitalism is now the dominant model worldwide. However, a number of tensions within it strongly affect corporate governance. These include:

- states' rights issues;
- federal/State tensions;
- declining productivity in the manufacturing sector since 1945;
- two hundred *plus* political parties (the two main parties are split into fifty states, each with their own pressures and priorities; it can be argued that each state variant has two wings – a presidential wing and a congressional wing);
- the Separation of Powers doctrine on which the American Constitution is based;
- regulatory power which is essentially state-based rather than federal.

Delaware has a judiciary very supportive to business in consequence and Delaware courts will respect 'directors' judgement' in virtually all but the most egregious cases (any action that shareholders wish to fight against a

Delaware-registered company or its officers has to be brought in a Delaware court and under Delaware law). The competition to emulate some of Delaware's laws led to the so-called 'race to the bottom'.

Characteristics of the USA corporate governance landscape

There is a basic apparent similarity to the UK:

- large well-developed capital market;
- diverse shareholder base;
- pensions mostly funded by stock market investment;
- heavy dominance of institutional funds;
- unitary boards;
- Anglo-Saxon common law basis for regulation.

But principal differences include:

- The agency problem is even more sharply defined.
- There is little 'follow-through' for regulatory power from the centre, which is blocked at the state line.
- The 'American Business Model' dominance aspires to be unfettered, untaxed and unregulated.
- Generally speaking, the corporate governance regime is more prescriptive than UK – especially after the Sarbanes-Oxley Act (see the next section).
- American companies often rely on increases in earnings to support the share price; shareholder returns therefore come through price appreciation in such cases.
- There is a legal requirement on managers and trustees of private pension funds to vote their holdings (Employment Retirement Income Security Act 1974).

As far as the detailed structure of governance is concerned, certain powers are reserved to the board, which has a duty of care and loyalty:

- the sale of the company or substantial assets;
- the declaration of dividends;
- a declaration of bankruptcy.

The Sarbanes-Oxley Act (also 'S-Ox' or 'SarbOx')

This act was introduced after the Enron scandal. Initially, a less prescriptive version was to be debated but the scandals immediately following

Enron – Tyco and WorldCom – toughened the legislation as it went through the US Senate. The Act's proper title – which is very rarely used – is the Public Company Accounting Reform and Investor Protection Act 2002. (Sarbanes-Oxley can work because it deals with public companies where shareholders are spread across the federal government's area. It may be the case in time that 'states-rightists' may challenge SarbOx in a conflict of laws.)

The Act is extensive in its powers and contains major provisions as follows:

1 *Integrity and completeness of financial reports* – the CEO and CFO of a listed company are required to assume personal responsibility for the company's financial reports by certifying that these

  • do not contain any untrue statement of material facts;
  • do not omit any material fact necessary to ensure that the statements are not misleading in the light of circumstances in which they are made;
  • fairly represent in all material respects the financial condition and results of the operations of the company.

2 *Non-interference in the audit process* – company directors, officers and anyone else acting at their direction are explicitly prohibited from interference in the audit process. Civil penalties are provided for such infringements

3 *PCAOB has been established* to register, inspect and discipline accounting firms. Also to set control standards – technical, quality, ethical and independence – relating to the preparation of audit reports.

4 *Audit independence* – the audit partner and review partner must vacate their positions after five years. It is illegal to offer specified non-audit services to audit clients. These include:

  • book-keeping;
  • design and implementation of financial control systems;
  • appraisal or valuation services;
  • actuarial services;
  • outsourced internal audit;
  • personnel functions;
  • brokering or dealing services;
  • investment advice or investment banking;
  • legal services;
  • expert services unrelated to audit;
  • any other service determined by PCAOB.
    All these stem directly from Enron.

5   *Company records* – it is now a criminal offence to alter, destroy, falsify, hide or shred a document or record to impede a criminal enquiry (also Enron).
6   *Whistleblowers* – audit committees are required to establish procedures for the protection of whistleblowers (Enron).
7   *Code of ethics* – companies are required to disclose whether they have codes of ethics for senior officers.

Following the passage of the Act, changes to the listing rules of both NYSE and the Nasdaq were introduced. These included mandatory votes by shareholders on remuneration policy; a requirement that a majority of the board be independent and a separation of the roles of CEO and chairman.

However, the financial collapse of 2007 occurred because Sarbanes-Oxley was not directed at the problems in the financial sector, nor at the behavioural issues which brought about the collapse.

The Act established the Public Company Accounting Oversight Board which is effectively the Act's police force. It has a number of significant characteristics, especially for those who cling to the belief that the USA is not a bureaucratic or interventionist society:

- It is highly intrusive in terms of its powers.
- It is extra-territorial.
- It is very well funded.

A comparison with the British FCA is salutary.

SarbOx attacked the accounting problem – *not* the market problem. In other words, it attacked only the techniques of the frauds which supported the larger intention to defraud.

- It has little new to say about shareholders rights.
- It makes the audit committee the client of the auditors – not the CFO.
- It may be overly prescriptive – there is some concern that even such minor matters as travel advances to executives may fall within the definition of loans to directors – which are now proscribed.
- It contains a provision for 'noisy withdrawal' by lawyers – who, if they resign, must disclose why they did so.
- It may even be over-powered – the penalties for comparatively low-level frauds have been raised from two years to fifteen years in jail.

American board structures are straightforward.

- They are unitary.
- They are composed of both executives and non-executives.

- They are committee led – with usually three major sub-committees: nomination, 'compensation' (remuneration) and audit.

Other significant prices of governance legislation include the Dodd-Frank Wall Street Reform and Consumer Protection Act which was passed during the Obama administration in 2010 as a response to the financial crisis of 2007–2008. This established a number of government agencies whose task it is to try to recognise instabilities in markets and stabilise them through action directly on major companies in the financial sectors. It brought about a structure similar to that of the agencies that were established in the UK after the financial crisis.

India

India is the world's largest democratically governed country by population. Its listed companies number roughly 10 000. Great strides have been made in the structures of governance over the past three decades. (Note: Western readers may find some of the Indian numerical units unfamiliar when reading about Indian companies. The Indian word 'crore' equals 10 million; 'lakh' stands for 100 000.)

The Confederation of Indian Industry issued a code of governance just before the May 1998 Asian currency collapse (brought about at root by the failure of the Russian currency). Although of a self-regulatory nature, it was accompanied by official exhortation and was at least as rigorous as in the UK. This was followed almost two years later by a code published by the Securities and Exchange Board of India which made more stringent requirements part of the listing process. It specified:

- One-tier boards (as stipulated by the Indian Companies Act 1956).
- Companies had to have a minimum of three directors.
- Only two types of shares were permitted for public companies – ordinary and preference; no multiple voting rights were allowed.
- Registration, reporting and dissolution/striking off were brought under a central company registrar system.
- The Indian equivalent of a US-style PCAOB was rejected in 2000 in favour of independent quality review boards.

The sequence of Indian corporate governance codes is as follows:

- Desirable Code of Corporate Governance 1998;
- Kumar Mangalam Birla Committee 2000;

- Naresh Chandra Committee on Corporate Audit 2002;
- Narayana Murthy Committee 2003.

The most recent iteration of governance principles is contained in the Companies Act 2013. This supplemented by or supports:

- Securities Contracts (Regulation) Act, 1956;
- Securities and Exchange Board of India Act, 1992;
- Securities and Exchange Board of India (Substantial Acquisition of Shares and Takeovers) Regulations, 2011 (the Takeover Code);
- Securities and Exchange Board of India (Prohibition of Insider Trading) Regulations, 2015;
- Securities and Exchange Board of India (Issue of Capital and Disclosure Requirements) Regulations, 2009;
- Depositories Act, 1996;
- Corporate Governance Voluntary Guidelines, 2009;
- National Voluntary Guidelines on Social, Environmental and Economic Responsibilities of Business, 2011;
- Guidelines on Corporate Social Responsibility and Sustainability for Central Public Sector Enterprises issued by the Department of Public Enterprises, Ministry of Heavy Industries and Public Enterprises (effective 1 April 2014 and applicable only to public sector enterprises).

Non-compliance with the provisions of the Companies Act on corporate governance can be punished with fines, imprisonment or both.

In June 2017 the Kotak Committee was established with the aim of improving standards of corporate governance of listed companies in India. It was charged with recommending measures that would

- ensure the independence of independent directors;
- improve safeguards and disclosures in respect of related party transactions;
- improve the effectiveness of board evaluation practices;
- improve the position of shareholders in matters of voting and participation in general meetings;
- improve disclosure and transparency related issues.

The committee's report was accepted in 2018 by the Securities and Exchange Board of India.

However, India still has substantial problems of corporate governance, related to sheer numbers; the preference for family and associate involvement; political cronyism; and the rickety taxation system.

Japan

The structure of the Japanese corporate economy is bound up with the *keiretsu* – associations of linked companies – that developed from the *zaibatsu* – the industrial holdings groups that were broken up after the Second World War. Both these structures are characterised by powerful family holdings.

In recent years, minority shareholders have begun to exercise more power – especially since the first hostile takeover bid (defeated) in early 2000 and the Shinsei bank affair. With the problems at Olympus and Toshiba and the Ghosn affair – which were rooted in long-term corruption by established managers – this has accelerated to the point where corporate governance is now one of the top subjects for study at Japanese business schools.

However, the momentum may be upset by the planned introduction by the Japanese trade ministry of a law (the Foreign Exchange and Foreign Trade Act) that requires pre-notification of a shareholding above 1% by a foreign investor in 'sensitive' industries. Japanese commentators fear that this may have a chilling effect on corporate activism, despite assurances by the Ministry that this is not what is intended.

The main business form in Japan is plc-style but with dual boards. However, there is no mandatory or automatic provision for employees to sit on the supervisory board. In 2001 the Japanese Corporate Governance Committee published a six-chapter, fourteen-point code which mixed shareholder and stakeholder views. The chapters deal with the following areas:

- the role and functions of the board;
- committees of the board;
- leadership and the CEO;
- shareholder rights and the shareholder litigation committee;
- fairness and transparency – internal control and disclosure;
- shareholder communication.

South Korea

The Korean equivalents of Japanese *keiretsu* are the *chaebols* which are similarly able to exercise power greater than their paper rights because of intricate cross-holdings. There is little regard for minority rights in Korean business activities.

The primary structure is plc-type, with a common law regime, unitary boards and only partial observance of legality with respect to minorities because of heavy family involvement. This has led to much corruption among the Korean business elite who may still tend to regard the companies that have a substantial public holding as 'their' companies – and act accordingly. In December 2019 eight employees from Samsung, one of the world's most recognisable brands, were found guilty of destroying evidence in a case linked to an alleged $3.9 billion accounting fraud that was linked to a plot to further entrench the control of the company's founding family.

In September 1999 the Korean Committee on Corporate Governance (a non-governmental committee) reported after six months' deliberation. Its principal recommendations were as follows:

- There should be equitable treatment of all shareholders.
- Company directors should act in the best interests of all shareholders, be appointed transparently through a nominating committee and with 25% being outsiders.
- Internal committees were to be established for audit, remuneration and operations.
- Stakeholders' interests should be considered in company strategies and policies.
- Company boards were to make key decisions and to operate with respect to the law.
- The corporate governance mode should be a 'comply or explain' regime for monitoring by the market.

The phrasing of some of the recommendations is significant in itself.

Hong Kong

In 2019 the Hong Kong Stock Exchange was the fourth largest in the world, and the third largest in Asia behind Tokyo and Shanghai. Since the change of administration after the expiry of the British lease in 1997, Hong Kong has been a Special Administrative Region of China. This is the basis of the 'One Country Two Systems' regime.

The regime is operated through a number of regulatory bodies, laws and codes. The regulatory bodies include:

- Financial Services and Treasury Bureau;
- Standing Committee on Company Law Reform;
- Companies Registry;
- Securities and Futures Commission;
- Hong Kong Exchanges and Clearing – holding company for SEHK;
- Hong Kong Monetary Authority – non-mandatory corporate governance guidelines for the banking industry;

- Hong Kong Institute of Directors;
- Hong Kong Institute of Chartered Secretaries;
- Hong Kong Securities Association.

Applicable laws include:

- Companies Ordinance and Amendment 2003 (deals with company formation, capital maintenance, financial and non-financial disclosure, administration, etc.);
- Securities and Futures Ordinance 2001;
- The Hong Kong Corporate Governance Code, the current version of which dates from 2004.

The first formal corporate governance initiative was launched in 1992, soon after the report of the Cadbury Commission (and while Hong Kong was still a British crown colony) when the SEHK introduced the Corporate Governance Project to enhance and promote a higher standard of corporate governance for Hong Kong's issuers. Influenced by international developments, the SEHK introduced its first Code of Best Practice in 1993. This first incarnation of the Code of Best Practice served as a non-mandatory guideline for issuers to devise their own codes of board practices. In the years that followed, Hong Kong's corporate governance regime evolved steadily. In 2005, following a lengthy consultation process from January 2002 to November 2004, the SEHK adopted the Code on Corporate Governance Practices in place of the Code of Best Practice. This included a new set of Listing Rules requiring issuers to include a corporate governance report in their annual reports. The code is based on a comply or explain regime. In its basic principles, the HK code is very similar to its UK counterpart.

In May 1998 the HK government required board committees to oversee each listed company's audit. At the time of the reform only 12 of the 600 listed companies had such a policy. The structure proposed came close to best practice in the West – committees would be chaired by outsiders but with executives participating.

In February 2000, the Pacific Economic Co-operation Council announced a further review. Hong Kong's record is better than many but was still poor in terms of insider dealing, protection of minorities and manipulation of accounts and information.

Characteristics of the HK company sector include the following:

- Heavy family domination of companies – estimated between 75% and 90%.
- Banks prohibited from share ownership (as 'substantial ownership of companies').

- Broadly similar to UK directorial obligations.
- Continuing tendency for one individual to be both chairman and chief executive.
- Remuneration is an issue.
- Audit committees are required by listing rules.
- Boards have between ten and twelve directors on average on HKEx – but there is a minimal number of NEDs for each company.

South Africa

In 1992 a committee on corporate governance was established in South Africa to deal with the problems of the shift of power to a representative state and the need for unification of the various races that live there. Chaired by Mervyn King, a South African judge, the committee reported in November 1994. This became known as 'King I' after the publication of a second report in 2002.

The code does not have the force of law. It revolves around the following characteristics:

- discipline;
- transparency;
- independence;
- accountability;
- responsibility;
- fairness;
- social responsibility.

Summary points of the report include:

- The implementation of a unitary board structure appropriate for South Africa.
- A mix of executive and non-executive directors.
- A definition of the responsibilities of the board.
- Balance of power considerations suggest that non-executives should be in the majority, with a transparent nominations committee consisting entirely of non-executives.
- The company secretary should be responsible for the induction and training of all new directors.
- Board meetings should be held at least every three months.
- There should be written terms of reference for board committees.
- A nominations committee should review the board itself every year.
- Non-executives should have access to the company's management without the executives being present.

- Performance-related pay should make up a large proportion of total remuneration for directors; however, options are less well-regarded than shares.
- Risk management should be a separate function of the audit committee.
- There should be a code of ethics for all stakeholders.
- External auditors should be independent of the company and its management.
- Sustainability reporting was to be implemented as soon as possible.
- Safety and occupational health maters should include consideration of the impact of HIV/AIDS.
- Environmental reporting was to be implemented as soon as possible.
- Social investment, including black economic empowerment, was to be a priority.
- 'Human capital development', including special provision for the training of women, was also a priority.

'King I' influenced the Commonwealth Association's recommendations in 1998. King II followed in 2002, taking into account the legislation that had been passed in the meantime.

Russia

Russia's implementation of corporate governance has been mixed up with the decline of the Soviet era, the rise of the oligarchy and a legal system that is still porous.

Prior to the collapse of the Soviet Union, the economy was controlled (supposedly) by policies promulgated by a mixture of the Politburo – the highest rank of the CPSU – and the Council of People's Commissars. Crudely, this is similar to a model that resembles the structure of a Parliament and a council of ministers. Economics and politics were closely intertwined.

Following the Russian Revolution, a state of civil war in Russia persisted until the early 1920s. The victory of the Bolsheviks led to the development of an economic system known as War Communism – a system of 'administrative-command' which was developed by a group of revolutionaries with no economic background – Lenin, Trotsky, Bukharin and Stalin. This structure eliminated any form of private enterprise, collectivised farms and controlled economic activity on an 'emergency' basis. (Soviet Union was surrounded by hostile States whose per capita incomes (even after war) were about 60% higher than hers.)

War Communism caused a state of economic collapse; it was supposedly money-less, market-less and property-less. It resulted in a flight from the cities, as the peasants refused to trade foodstuffs and the industrial work-ers could find nothing to eat. It was replaced by the New Economic Policy, seized upon by Stalin after his victory in the struggle to succeed Lenin. This employed 'scientific socialism' to allocate resources according to perceived need – "from each according to his ability; to each according to his need". It also destroyed the peasant base as an act of revenge for what was seen as the sabotage of the initial system by the 'kulaks' – the wealthy peasant sub-class.

Essentially this structure continued until the collapse of the USSR in 1991, with regular revisions of Five-Year Plans which controlled outputs and dictated growth. The plans were prepared by Gosplan (the State Plan-ning Commission); production was the responsibility of individual min-istries which supervised state enterprises and collective farms. Primary features of this style of control were:

- There was no 'rational economic calculator' for the deployment of resources in the absence of a price system which attempted to equate supply and demand objectively.
- No one individual in a position of intermediate power could make more than a very few decisions, because of the complexity of the system.
- Huge conflicts of individuals' responsibilities and multiple loci of power.
- Massive body of regulations (to supplant the laws of economics).
- No general rules – they would have interfered with the authority of individuals to intervene.
- Arbitrary, incompetent decision-making.
- Low-level equilibrium resulted; a condition of 'stasis plus'.
- Huge bureaucracy.
- Continual shortages of all goods.
- Substantial black markets, and 'just-in-case' opportunism in the hoard-ing of goods and resources.
- Massive amounts of embezzlement by state employees.

But the system did bring the USSR from economic backwardness to mili-tary superpower in two generation and managed to survive sixty years – at least seven economic cycles.

In 1985 Mikhail Gorbachev assumed power and introduced *glasnost* (open-ness) and *perestroika* (reform) to try to overcome structural weaknesses. At the same time, Boris Yeltsin assumed power in central Russia and decided to challenge the Soviet Union. He instructed all Russian banks to withhold tax payments made by Russian State enterprises to the USSR budget. As a con-sequence, the Soviet Union collapsed. Since the Union had printed more and more money to pay its expenditures instead of using the locked-up tax funds, there was a huge monetary 'overhang' in the Russian economy.

There were two ways of mopping this up: either import consumer goods bought from the West using Western loans (Gorbachev's preference); or issue assets in return for the cash to encourage investment – in other words, privatisation of State assets.

Prices were de-controlled, impoverishing the ordinary population; those in control of assets benefited hugely. Privatisation then became a give-away; many in the population, hungry for basic necessities, traded their holdings for cash for food, or did not understand what 'shares' represented.

Yeltsin was advised by economists trained in the West who had witnessed the popularity of privatisations; the leaders of the Red enterprises were well represented in Parliament and using their power to demand concessions from Yeltsin, privatisation was adapted to benefit insiders.

Banks lent the State (its own) money locked up from tax receipts which it was illegal to pass over to the Union. The Mafia begin to infiltrate senior industrial positions; organisations of veterans of the Afghan and Chechen wars – the so-called 'athletic clubs' – and the KGB all begin to position themselves for economic power. By 1994, the Russian Government estimated there were forty thousand criminally controlled enterprises in Russia – two thousand of which were in the State sector.

In managerial terms, this led to the following:

* The criminal form of enterprise became the norm.
* Criminal enterprises levied taxes (protection); ran security services and had their own administrative systems; they colonised legitimate activity and took it over.
* Criminality gradually morphed into 'normality' on a State-wide platform.
* The State legal superstructure was maintained as in the command economy but penalties for transgression became even more severe.
* Regulations were dispensable.
* The principal-agent problem became both muted (for the majority) – and more acute (for a small number) and irrelevant for society as a whole.
* Prices reflected demand and supply but in a very specialised way – for a limited range of discretionary goods.
* Secondary economic signals (like queues, complaints, waiting lists, the black market) disappeared or became irrelevant.
* Barter became more significant than black markets.

Democracy needed a pluralistic dispersion of power to maintain itself, so Putin began his attack on the oligarchs, dispersing power but with the intention not of democratising, but of neutralising and re-centralising.

In corporate governance terms, the situation may now have stabilised. Company structure has two basic forms:

* ZAO – closed-end joint stock companies (similar to 'Ltd')
* OAO – open-end joint stock companies (similar to 'plc')

The Russian 'company charter' equates to articles

Companies are characterised by senior managers controlling significant levels of equity (not necessarily through direct ownership). Separation of ownership and control is very limited: there is little investment and little bank lending to corporations (most large businesses generate their own working and development capital – or use state funds illegally to do so). Protection of minority shareholders is poor. There are rudimentary controls on pre-emption, some minority protection from forfeiture, some dividend protection, some protection for general meetings, some strictures on disclosure and related party transactions.

Regulation is undertaken through the Federal Commission on the Securities Market which was established in 1994 – subsequently renamed the Federal Service for Financial Markets (2004). Its functions are as follows:

* oversees market operations;
* licences activity;
* collects information on market operations;
* drafts and manages the Russian Corporate Governance code;
* runs training courses.

Governance requires disclosure against a 'comply or disclose and explain' rule.

Board structure

Every corporate entity must have a single person executive – the General Director. ZAOs and OAOs may also have a management board. The GD reports to the supervisory board and to the shareholders in general meeting. Some recent trends to move towards Western-style board operations away from concentrating power in the hands of the GD. Supervisory board directors are usually not less than five in number with gradations depending on company size (according to shareholder numbers). The supervisory board is theoretically very powerful – a council of shareholders and shareholders have theoretical power to alter all these arrangements on demand.

The most recent iteration of the Corporate Governance Code was made in 2014. The European Bank for Reconstruction and Development classed Russian corporate governance as relatively sound but noted:

- a lack of transparency in company management;
- a lack of accountability to shareholders;
- unfair treatment of minorities;
- a weak co-ordination among shareholders;
- a weak corporate governance culture;
- poor enforcement of laws and regulations.

Disclosure issues

Companies must be audited by law and must have an audit ('revision') committee.

Shareholder rights

Common shares and preference shares are the only types available, but fractional shares may be held.

7 The future of corporate governance

The Future: that period of time in which our affairs prosper, our friends are true and our happiness is assured.

Ambrose Bierce: The Devil's Dictionary (1911)

The preceding chapters have shown that there are still myriad problems for corporate governance to deal with – mostly centred around the risks that the parties to the governance contract are willing to assume and the rewards that they expect to achieve.

The intensity of corporate governance debate probably reached its peak in the years immediately before the financial crisis came to a head in 2007–2008. This is hardly surprising, since in many ways the numerous failures of corporate governance precipitated the crisis. It is, therefore, completely understandable that discussion about what was going wrong was intense just before the collapse.

What is surprising, though, is the way that the debate has flagged in the decade (and more) since then. If the corporate governance debate was intense in the first seven or eight years of the twenty-first century, then that implies that the issues raised by the debate were still a work in progress. But in the UK at least, in the decade of austerity that followed the near-collapse of the finance sector, there has been little significant progress in tackling the issues that were identified in the numerous reports and reviews published or undertaken between 1992 and 2005, about controlling pay, making companies more responsive and re-balancing the gender weighting on company boards. The reports that were conducted into the problems and causes of the 2007–2008 crisis were usually too late to have any effect or so anodyne as to be of little remedial value (the Walker Report and the Bank of England Enquiry). Work in progress has become an abandoned building site.

To be fair, in the UK there was the beginning of a co-ordinated legal structure (in the shape of the Companies Act 2006; the Corporate Manslaughter and Corporate Homicide Act of 2007; and the Bribery Act of 2010) which began to tackle the problem of the 'controlling mind' problem and associated issues of corporate responsibility. With the passing of the Criminal Finances Act 2017, the legal structure became equipped with sanctions to compel proper behaviour, which had been threatened with the passage of the Bribery Act (but which has only been employed so far to prosecute cases that could have been dealt with under pre-existing legislation).

The years after the collapse were absorbed with debate about the public finances, which obscured questionable issues about companies' financial and behavioural governance. When 'scandals' did occur, they were tangled up in public financing problems or policies – the Persimmon bonus scandal (and the Buy-to-Let housing policy); the collapse, or near collapse, of several companies (Carillion; Interserve; Serco and Kier) supplying services to the public sector in the 'out-sourcing' scandals which were implemented, supposedly, to reduce costs. Then, for three years after 2016, almost everything in the political world became subordinated to debate about Brexit.

Because of this, old problems have not been solved. But unfortunately, new ones are coming fast towards us – and little preparation has been made for them.

The first chapter ended with a suggestion that other issues than the purely mechanistic might be incorporated into a description of corporate governance in terms of its purpose:

'Corporate governance is really about holding the balance between economic and social goals and between individual and communal goals. The aim is to as nearly as possible align the interests of individuals, corporations and society (*Cadbury*).'

Taking that as a benchmark, some of the other issues that corporate governance will have to deal with are set out in this chapter. Many of these problems are of a different nature from those that deal solely with the relationships between the 'traditional' parties to the governance relationship described by Cadbury. With a new form of economy taking shape in the early years of the twentieth century – where the primary (extractive), secondary (manufacturing) and tertiary (service-based) sectors are being overtaken in economic and social significance by an 'info-tainment' industry – the problems are shifting increasingly towards the relationship between the company and society.

With the growth of new data-based technologies, companies are upending the relationship between themselves and customers, so that the customer now becomes the supplier of raw material in the form of data about their personal preferences and habits. This is then sold on as 'product" to other companies.

Size of companies

The size, scope and power of companies has increased regularly and consistently. Some companies now have economic power that exceeds that of small nation states. Their power to challenge political priorities is now being enhanced through devices such as those incorporated in some trade treaties – known as Investor-State Dispute Settlement, where companies can take states to court if they believe that their economic activity has been circumscribed and their potential markets curtailed – *by politically determined priorities* (which are of course usually things that voted have decided upon).

Company and state – issues of power

Many companies now supply services to individuals that have become critical to individual well-being and economic activity – and are so large and so complicated that they are 'too big to regulate'. Laws designed to regulate libel and the public interest in the nineteenth and early twentieth centuries cannot cope with the complexity, scope and pervasiveness of these companies, which now mix entertainment, information and data collection. The problems with this economic development – into a stage of economic activity beyond the tertiary economy, where the customer becomes the raw material of the company's output – have been well-illustrated by the debate over the regulation of Facebook and its potential to interfere in political processes throughout the world.

Company and state – instruments of policy

The use of private sector businesses to pursue the aims of government – usually overtly but sometimes covertly – has a long history. The Astra and Matrix Churchill cases of the 1980s are two particularly relevant instances.

More recently, the problems of encrypted messaging on mobile phones have been the subject of heated debate in the past few years. Proponents of civil liberties defend the rights of companies to produce such products, while governments have resented the use of messaging services to which they have no access, which might carry messages between criminals or terrorists. Some shareholders might have bought into the companies on the basis that their proprietary products offered them a commercial advantage which made them more profitable. Should those shareholders be disadvantaged when governments decide to force the companies to 'open up' encryption and then possibly use that lever to demand more concessions, further reducing the commercial value of the companies?

The internet

The facilitator of much of the acceleration of change in the governance of companies is the internet. Companies can now exist in an environment for which there is little established regulatory structure and where the imposition of such structures is looked upon variously as insidious or authoritarian.

Technological change

The use of super-computers in investment strategies and execution is an area fraught with problems for regulators – who will always be on the back foot as far as developments are concerned, reacting to changes in market strategies and operations brought about by more sophisticated technology. Some examples of these problems have already been given. More will develop as technological change increases the ability of traders to gain an advantage over their competitors, using fair means or otherwise.

Artificial intelligence will almost certainly pose problems for regulators, employees and shareholders. We have already seen that the use of highly sophisticated algorithms has produced turmoil in some share markets – so-called flash-crashes where lots of different factors combining to spook automated trading systems have become events that have occurred two or three times a decade. Self-righting mechanisms in the algorithms appear to make the market recover quickly, but during the time that it is not stable (however short that may be), some parties will be winners and some will be losers. These limited forms of artificial intelligence – limited by both their range of application and their ability – still 'think' (perform logical functions) and behave (execute actions) many times faster than the humans that created them are able to do. What happens when artificial intelligence is extended beyond the financial sector into manufacturing and services? Preliminary steps have been taken in some legal matters (house conveyancing, for instance) and even dispute resolution by arbitration. Anywhere rules can be applied is potentially an operating ground for AI. Yet even skilled humans make mistakes when applying rules. How will companies be dealt with that make extensive use of AI when that AI goes on to make mistakes that may result in substantial economic loss to a customer, supplier or neighbour? Or when something happens that causes death of an employee or an innocent by-stander? Who will be the controlling mind that can be identified then?

Controlling mind

This issue has never been properly resolved by corporate governance theory policies or even legislation (despite the start made by the authorities in the UK). In the context of the five points covered, it becomes even more pressing that a legal framework is put in place to separate the innocent shareholders from being punished by the deliberate transgressions or culpable negligence of derelict directors who operate a company in such a way that it commits significant crimes.

Principle and spirit versus letter of the law regulation

Those states which operate an Anglo-Saxon legal process tend to favour principle as the method of controlling companies, while codified jurisdictions tend to prefer legalistic solutions. The gaps between laws and activities and between principles and behaviour is where issues contrary to good governance flourish – like weeds colonising the gaps in between paving stones. With the mobility offered by the internet, companies can avoid the strictures of one jurisdiction while operating in another. The problem that used to plague companies – the 'clash of laws', where two jurisdictions might hold completely different views on matters of legal principle – has been replaced by the silence of laws, internationally.

Inadequate regulation

In most cases where scandals later come to light, the process of regulation has been dependent on the scrutiny of information provided by the companies themselves. The malpractice usually comes to light only when a whistleblower informs of the company's misbehaviour or when something goes so wrong that it can no longer be concealed (see the earlier sections on '"The Controlling Mind" Problem' and 'Outright Criminality' in Chapter 2).

Increasingly complex and diversified companies may well exacerbate this problem, which will ultimately be solved only by more investment in regulation, which companies and shareholders may well find intrusive and will certainly cause political disputes.

Complexity of environment – climate change: sustainability

The next major area of contention in the public view of companies is almost certainly to be in the issues of sustainability and climate change.

In August 2019, an American organisation, the Business Round Table, suggested that companies should move away from a fixed focus on only bettering the shareholder and extend their horizons to thinking about necessary improvements in their priorities regarding the treatment of their employees and social inequality. Predictably, the wording and presentation of the announcement was seen as largely cosmetic by many pressure groups – especially since it appeared to suggest that the purpose of the recommendation was to head off rising populism rather than be a fundamental shift in a business paradigm.

Founders' shares

In recent years many companies' prospectuses have revealed that the founders of companies who are offering their shares in a flotation will not relinquish control of the company. In fact quite the opposite often happens, with founders' shares being incorporated in the shareholding structure but giving vastly preferential rights. Such devices turn the concept of limited liability on its head. The examples of WeWork and Facebook are particularly striking. The theory of these developments (rather than a partial argument for them) has yet to be written – and, apart from being based on overweening arrogance and greed, appears to have little coherent theoretical justification.

Employee 'empowerment' and governance internalisation

It may seem odd to suggest that employees might pose a problem for governance. The term used for the heading for this section usually means the exact opposite of what it says – frequently employees are not truly given increasing latitude in decision-making but are merely burdened with more responsibility when things go wrong. But in some industries – especially the knowledge-based industries where advanced conceptual skills are the motor for the development of companies – employees can be become crucially significant 'mini-entrepreneurs'.

The old concept of industrial activity was that finance (capital) and labour (employees) were brought together by entrepreneurs (who had some visionary intention) to form companies that then produced profit shared in some proportion between the three parties. In the modern world the position of the traditional entrepreneur – at the centre of the web, controlling the use of (passive) labour – is not quite so clear-cut. Labour is often not passive, and capital is often quite vocal; strains are often set up between the two, and in directions that might not be expected. A good example of this is the actions of Google employees in respect of Google's 'Dragonfly' project. It appears from the limited amount of information that leaked from the company that a project to develop a special search engine that would comply with China's heavily state-censored internet was torpedoed by engineers working on the project. This form of self-governance is unusual, and as concerns about ethical behaviour – the use of industrial toxins, plastic production, climate-damaging activity and so on – increase, governance issues may become more internalised to (some) companies rather than externally imposed.

Cultural issues – the purpose of shares in listed companies

With companies now able to have access to many different forms of funding, the purposes of listing a company's shares are not quite as clear as they once were.

The initial influx of money on flotation or listing may well boost a company's cash resources. But it may equally allow founder shareholders to cash in their shares, which are otherwise only notionally valuable, with little or no money going to the company.

The model of the limited liability company, which floats its shares in order to further its business, dating from the nineteenth century has come under criticism in the second decade of the twenty-first.

Some critics (for instance, Colin Mayer et al) have suggested that the model for the founding shareholders to retain their voting influence while selling non-voting shares to later shareholders, and to benefit from those sales, is a far better model for providing for good companies to grow further, be sustained and maintained rather than gobbled up by acquisitive, voracious competitors. (This behaviour is indulging in what came to be known as 'Cakeism' during the Brexit debate.) The companies are immune from being taken off the market before their peak is reached because the super-shares owned by the founders who stay on board, and in control, effectively prevent a takeover from occurring.

The counters to this argument are not hard to see and are difficult for the Cakeists to deflect. What exactly is the purpose of floated companies under the Cakeist scheme, if it is not to raise capital for the company? (The answer is fairly obvious.) Will large companies with founders having operational control not simply become like Facebook and Amazon – just super-gobblers of smaller quoted companies? Amazon and Facebook have a history of buying up new technologies for incorporation in their own empires before the technologies are fully formed. Will this do the economy any good in the long run? With no shareholder input to restrain or control them, will companies with founders with bloated self-images (see the WeWork prospectus describing the qualities of the founder) allocate resources efficiently in societal terms? How does succession occur in such a business? Under the law of unintended consequences – having founders in control, repelling any form of market discipline – might those companies not simply act in a manner towards other smaller companies which the corporate Cakeists hope to avoid? Are the few large companies immune from takeover, deciding the allocation of resources healthy for a democratic political system?

One of the precepts of the capitalist model has been that of creative destruction – the market deals with companies that do not innovate or cannot move fast enough by having them absorbed or destroyed by competitors. The market is supposed to find the best allocation of resources – although the claims for this effect are generally overstated. But will an economic structure composed of a few giant quoted companies run by, dominated by and controlled by a few individuals allocate resources any better?

All these questions have yet to be effectively dealt with. There may be satisfactory answers, but at the moment the governance issues are largely unexplored and the theory is unmapped.

The issues quoted above are 'known unknowns', to quote a piece of early twenty-first-century obfuscation from American politics. We cannot deal with the 'unknown unknowns' in corporate governance any more than in any other area. Yet they are the ones which bite the hardest. The Cadbury formulation for 'corporate governance' is not up to the task to determine what these unknowns might be.

8 Conclusion

Drawing the strands of the previous chapters together with the suggestions for future developments made in the last one, a few concluding statements can be used to summarise significant issues.

Until the last decade of the century, what we now term corporate governance had been subject mostly to developments in case law in the Anglo-Saxon legal jurisdictions where common law was the predominant structure of legal regulation.

The later part of the twentieth century saw a rapid increase in the social visibility and social significance of issues now defined as 'corporate governance'. This was a worldwide phenomenon, emphasising the dominance of the capitalist model and the many variants on the limited liability company. In the UK it revolved around issues of pay and the perceived unequal behaviour accorded to 'bosses' in comparison to 'workers', but the underlying roots were much deeper. In other countries, corporate governance reforms sought to address different issues including basic issues of corporate transparency, probity in reporting, and shareholders' rights.

The first attempt to define corporate governance, made in the report of the 1992 Cadbury Committee, has so far stood as its most universal description, despite the serious flaws in its formulation and applicability. After the Cadbury initiatives, a system of governance that operates by principle rather than rule, of requiring compliance *or* explanation and of exhortation rather than compulsion still exists in the UK. However, underneath these 'soft' structures lie a quartet of legal powers which form a coherent structure and can be used collectively to compel action:

- the Companies Act 2006;
- the Corporate Manslaughter and Corporate Homicide Act 2007;
- the Bribery Act 2010;
- the Criminal Finances Act 2017.

This web of laws arose despite the hiatus in reforms brought about by the crisis in financial structures that occurred in 2007–2008 and which lasted for a decade. The crisis had itself been brought about a failure in the wider concepts of corporate governance – but from the societal view rather than the narrow company-based view. It was accelerated by the rapid development of 'finance capitalism' in the advanced economies as they moved away from the primary and secondary industries and increasingly into the tertiary and further – into complex variants of that stage.

Worldwide, many challenges to effective corporate governance remain. Many countries have cultural obstacles to the transparent operation of companies: family ties; legal structures; inadequate application of the rule of law; the weakness of central governments; taxation systems; corruption; social division; and pronounced income inequality.

The rise of concerns about the sustainability of economic activity will place further pressure on companies to absorb principles of good governance and to demonstrate that they have applied those principles to their operations. At the same time, the increasing complexity of the business environment in which companies operate will produce a number of challenges to corporate governance over the next decade.

The analytical paradigms that the Cadbury definition provides will prove unequal to the task for developing corporate governance further: the flexibility and lack of prescription that was touted as its strength, will be its primary weakness. New paradigms will have to be developed that involve examination of company behaviour along at least four dimensions:

1 *Procedural* – does the company have systems which bring about the ends desired by shareholders in a fair, transparent and legal way which are not subject to distortion by managers?
2 *Structural* – is the company set up in such a way that, once these priorities have been determined by shareholders, they are effectively executed throughout the company?
3 *Behavioural* – does the company act in a way that the first two dimensions are respected, or is it a case of managerial action perverting the company's objectives, either openly or discreetly?
4 *Systemic* – is the wider governance environment (sponsored, controlled and policed by the regulatory authorities) conducive to proper observance of the other dimensions?

The challenge to existing corporate governance systems will probably be from all of the problematic areas listed. Although the thrust of reform diminished after the financial crisis, the problems have not gone away.

As well as the old risk/reward problem, the progress of very large companies into areas where information and entertainment blend provides a further area of risk for societies becoming increasingly dependent on electronic systems of communication. These turn the customer–company relationship on its head. Customers used to be at one end of the company's production cycle. Now they are at both *simultaneously* as the world enters a fourth stage of economic development – beyond extractive, beyond manufacturing and beyond service-based.

Customers are now raw material as well as consumers. They supply details of their habits, their movements, their friendships and their political opinions to companies which then process them and 'monetise' them. This trend will provide the greatest challenge to corporate governance in years to come.

Appendix
Accounting and corporate scandals

UK accounting and corporate scandals, 2000–2015 – an incomplete but representative list

- John Ho Park (1999; Griffin Trading; London) – disastrous bets on German futures market closed a clearing platform.
- Equitable Life (2000) – the guaranteed annuity scandal.
- Administration of Turner and Newell (2001) – pension fund deficit of £400 million.
- Qinetiq privatisation (2002) – civil servants both negotiated and benefited from privatisation.
- Royal Dutch Shell reserves restatement (2004) – extensive misleading statements.
- Actis Capital and CDC (2004) – excessive remuneration.
- Langbar International (2005) – AIM listed 'pump and dump' fraud.
- BP Texas City blast (2005) – cost-cutting reduces maintenance expenditure and leads to lethal explosions.
- BAe ethics report (Woolf Report – 2008) – *el-Yamama* scandal; systemically corrupt business.
- RBS/ABN Amro (2007) – failed due diligence on acquisition that precipitated collapse of RBS.
- Northern Rock failure (2008) – the start of the 2007–2008 financial crisis brought about by a flawed business model.
- Sirbir Energy (2009) – mismanagement of AIM-listed public company by a major Russian shareholder.
- Carphone Warehouse (2009) – director's loans scandal.
- JJB Sports (2009) – director's loans; significant governance lapses.
- Keydata (2009) – improper accounting.
- Farepak (2009) – loss of Christmas savings funds.
- The Phoenix 4–Leyland (2009) – preferential terms for directors on collapse.

- Arch Cru failure (2009) – investment fund fraud, supposedly low risk; subsequent mismanagement by administrators and by FSCS.
- Mitchells and Butler (2009–) – financial engineering that lost shareholders £1 billion to £4 billion.
- Weavering Capital (2009) – hedge fund failure brought about by fraud.
- The PPI Scandals (all UK banks).
- LIBOR manipulation (all UK banks).
- FOREX manipulation (all UK banks).
- Money laundering (several UK banks, but especially HSBC and Standard Chartered).
- Tesco profits overstatement (2014) – dubious accounting practices.
- Sports Direct (2016) – wages unlawfully withheld; poor employment conditions; governance breaches.
- Carillion (2017 and continuing) – and the near-collapse of other outsourcing companies.
- Cambridge Analytica (2018 and continuing) – Facebook data and the rigging of UK parliamentary elections.
- Patisserie Valerie (2018) – grossly incompetent directorial oversight.
- Ted Baker (2018) – sexual harassment claims and profits collapse.
- BhS (2018) – continuing saga of the collapse of the Philip Green empire.
- Kier (2019) – break-up of the construction company because of poor directorial control over two years.
- The 'MeToo' scandals – numerous instances of sexual harassment, particularly in the UK in retail – Harrods, Ted Baker and Arcadia (Philip Green) – and entertainment companies – especially those owned by Harvey Weinstein.
- Crossrail overspend – failure of board oversight of contractor controls.
- HS2 overspend – failure of board control; land purchasing imbalance; flawed forecasting.
- PwC (2019) – professional incompetence; partnership fined £4.55 million and two partners fined £140 000 each over failures in audits, including listed company Redcentric.
- KPMG – bullying culture (2019); partners reprimanded or moved.
- Woodford Equity Income Fund (2019) – collapse of the 'Patient Capital' fund because of mis-stated risk profile of fund; inadequate performance of the Authorised Corporate Director; promotion of fund by a broker insufficiently objective because of fee income.
- SwedBank (2019) – Baltic money-laundering scandal.
- Danske Bank (2019) – Baltic money-laundering scandal.
- Kraft Heinz (2019) – material mis-statement of past accounts.

- Southern Water (Greensands Investments) (2019) – UK company fined £125 million for deliberately falsifying monitoring information and misleading customers.
- The collapse of Thomas Cook (2019) – directors pay; consultancy costs; over-indebtedness.

Audit failures: an incomplete list – worldwide

- ZZZZ Best; 1986; Ernst & Whinney; United States. Ponzi scheme run by Barry Minkow.
- Barlow Clowes; 1988; Deloitte United Kingdom.
- MiniScribe; 1989; Coopers & Lybrand; United States. False invoicing.
- Bank of Credit and Commerce International; 1991; Pricewaterhouse-Coopers/Ernst & Whinney; United Kingdom.
- Phar-Mor; 1992; Coopers & Lybrand; United States mail fraud, wire fraud, bank fraud, and transportation of funds obtained by theft or fraud; losses estimated at $1 billion.
- Informix Corporation; 1996; Ernst & Young; United States.
- Wickes; 1996; Arthur Andersen; UK; losses concealed.
- Sybase; 1997; Ernst & Young; United States.
- Cendant; 1998; Ernst & Young; United States.
- Waste Management, Inc; 1999; Arthur Andersen; United States. Financial mis-statements.
- MicroStrategy; 2000; PricewaterhouseCoopers; United States.
- Unify Corporation; 2000; Deloitte & Touche; United States.
- Computer Associates; 2000; KPMG; United States. Massive frauds to inflate share price.
- Xerox; 2000; KPMG; United States. Falsifying financial results.
- One.Tel; 2001; Ernst & Young; Australia.
- Enron; 2001; Arthur Andersen; United States.
- Adelphia; 2002; Deloitte & Touche; United States. Milking of company funds by founders.
- AOL; 2002; Ernst & Young; United States. Inflated sales.
- Bristol-Myers Squibb; 2002; PricewaterhouseCoopers; United States. Inflated sales.
- CMS Energy; 2002; Arthur Andersen; United States. 'Round trip' trades.
- Duke Energy; 2002; Deloitte & Touche; United States. 'Round trip' trades.
- Dynegy; 2002; Arthur Andersen; United States. 'Round trip' trades.
- El Paso Corporation; 2002; Deloitte & Touche; United States. 'Round trip' trades.

- Freddie Mac; 2002; PricewaterhouseCoopers; United States. Understated earnings.
- Global Crossing; 2002; Arthur Andersen; Bermuda. Network capacity swaps to inflate revenues.
- Halliburton; 2002; Arthur Andersen. United States. Improper booking of cost overruns.
- Homestore.com; 2002; PricewaterhouseCoopers; United States. Improper booking of sales.
- Kmart; 2002; PricewaterhouseCoopers; United States. Misleading accounting practices.
- Mirant; 2002; KPMG; United States. Overstated assets and liabilities.
- Nicor; 2002; Arthur Andersen; United States. Overstated assets, understated liabilities.
- Peregrine Systems; 2002; KPMG; United States. Overstated sales.
- Qwest Communications; 1999, 2000, 2001, 2002; Arthur Andersen; October 2002 KPMG; United States. Inflated revenues.
- Reliant Energy; 2002; Deloitte & Touche; United States. 'Round trip' trades.
- Sunbeam; 2002; Arthur Andersen; United States.
- Tyco International; 2002; PricewaterhouseCoopers; Bermuda. Improper accounting.
- WorldCom; 2002; Arthur Andersen; United States. Overstated cash flows.
- Royal Ahold; 2003; Deloitte & Touche; United States. Inflating promotional allowances.
- Parmalat; 2003; Grant Thornton Spa; Italy. Falsified accounting documents.
- HealthSouth Corporation; 2003; Ernst & Young; United States.
- Chiquita Brands International; 2004; Ernst & Young; United States. Illegal payments.
- AIG; 2004; PricewaterhouseCoopers; United States. Accounting of structured financial deals.
- MG Rover; 2005; Deloitte; UK. Deliberate disregard of professional ethics.
- BAE; 1997–2007; KPMG; audit failure in respect of bribes and concealment of subsidiaries; case dropped by FRC as outdated.
- Bernard L. Madoff Investment Securities LLC; 2008; Friehling & Horowitz; United States.
- Anglo Irish Bank; 2008; Ernst & Young; Ireland. Hidden loans controversy.
- Satyam Computer Services; 2009; PricewaterhouseCoopers; India. Falsified accounts.

- Cattles plc; 2009 PwC; KPMG; Deloitte; UK. Creditors mounting action for recovery of £1.6 billion.
- Lehman Brothers; 2010; Ernst & Young; United States. Failure to disclose Repo 105 transactions to investors.
- Sino-Forest Corporation; 2011; Ernst & Young; Canada-China. Asset loss or non-existence.
- Olympus Corporation; 2011; Ernst & Young; Japan 'Tobashi' frauds using acquisitions.
- Autonomy Corporation; 2012; Deloitte & Touche; United States. Accounting problems in acquisition.
- Quinn Insurance; 2010; PriceWaterhouseCoopers; Ireland. Case pending.
- Vincent Tchenguiz (via the SFO) 2012; Grant Thornton; UK excerpt from judge's comments: "Its conduct has repeatedly crossed the line from proper ethical practice into areas of ethical, civil and potentially criminal wrongdoing".
- Penn West Exploration/Obsidian; 2013. Over-indebted and accounting irregularities.
- Pescanova; 2014. Understated debt.
- Petrobras – the Car Wash scandals (continuing).
- Monte dei Paschi de Siena; 2013–2016. Hidden losses concealed by management.
- Toshiba; 2015. Profits discovered to have been overstated for at least three years.
- Valeant Pharmaceuticals – drug price fixing and insider dealing.
- Odebrecht – see Petrobras.
- 1MDB Malaysia; 2015 and continuing. Theft of $3.5 billion from state-owned development fund while run by Minister of Finance Incorporated [*sic*].
- BhS – collapse of department store chain, shaky finances revealed after sale by Philip Green.
- Carillion – collapse of UK outsourcing company.
- KPMG partner struck off list of auditors and fined after admitting six charges of misconduct in relation to South African Gupta family company audits.

Further reading

Textbooks

There is a plethora of books available as textbooks for students of corporate governance, which takes the subject in more detail than this brief volume.

However, many are written by academic authors who have little practical experience of the subject. Interested readers who want more explanation should look for one of the following:

Bloomfield, S: The Theory and Practice of Corporate Governance; Cambridge; 2013

Tricker, R: Corporate Governance: Principles, Policies, and Practices; OUP; 2019

Although it is now getting dated, the following is an excellent review of a number of theoretical and legal issues:

Parkinson, J E: Corporate Power and Responsibility; OUP; 1995

Original material, legislation and commentaries

The Cadbury Report – downloadable from the Judge Business School website
The Companies Act 2006; available as a download from legislation.gov.uk
PwC: A Practical guide to the Companies Act 2006; Walters Kluwer; 2010

One of the best ways to learn about the practical implications of corporate governance practice – good and bad—is to watch films and read popularised 'case studies' and biographies. A small selection of the best is set out below:

Films:

Wall Street
Inside job
The Corporation
Enron: The Smartest Guys in the Room
Margin Call
A Crude Awakening

'Case Studies'

About Matrix Churchill:

Henderson P: The Unlikely Spy; Bloomsbury; 1993

About The Astra Affair:

James, G: In the Public Interest; Warner 1995

A French case study

Johnson, J and Orange, M: The Man who Tried to buy the World; Penguin; 2003

About trading

Lewis, M: Flash Boys; Penguin; 2013
Lewis, M: Liar's Poker; Hodder; 2006
Augar, P: Chasing Alpha; Vintage 2010
Augar, P: Barclays – the bank that Lived a Little; Allen Lane; 2018

Theory

And for those readers who are *really* keen
Albert, M: Capitalism against Capitalism; Whurr; 1992
Hilferding, R: Finance Capitalism; Routledge; 2007
Schumpeter, J: Capitalism Socialism and Democracy; Routledge 2010.

Glossary (by point of introduction)

Shares

A share is a specific portion of the total capital of a company. The owners of shares may be entitled to a number of privileges which usually include the right to the payment of dividends and the right to vote at general meetings on proposals (once passed, these proposals are known as 'resolutions').

The minimum privileges and obligations are defined in statute in the UK and are set out for each company in the 'Articles of Association', which give details of rights and entitlements beyond the statutory minimum.

The most significant characteristic of shares is that they are *perpetual*. Except under very specific circumstances, they exist independently of specific shareholders. This means they can be bought and sold, traded and pledged as collateral. In the UK they may be cancelled only with the permission of the High Court.

There are numerous types of shares, the names of which may indicate the possession of certain rights. The most common type is the '*ordinary share*'. Private companies can have a variety of share types in addition to 'ordinaries'. These might offer *convertibility* (the right to change in ordinary shares at some specified time or on some event), *redeemability* (the right to demand repayment of the shares at some point, provided the overall value of the share capital is not reduced) and *cumulatión* (the right to accumulate dividends that the company may not be able to pay in any one year, to be paid at some later date). If the entitlements of the shares are not honoured, then the powers of those shareholders to influence the company's policies and behaviour will be greatly enhanced.

So, in loose terms, shareholders 'own' the company in which they hold shares; but in practical terms, this ownership right is highly circumscribed, especially for companies which have their shares traded on a recognised public exchange.

Articles of association

An obligatory document which sets out the contract between shareholders, the company and its directors. The minimum terms are defined in statute in the UK (Companies Act 2006). As well as describing the mechanisms of the company's operations – types and rights of shares, annual meeting arrangements, matters concerning directorial appointments and directors' powers – the document will typically include clauses that deal with the borrowing powers of the company and with anti-dilution provisions to ensure that existing shareholders do not have their shareholdings whittled away by stealth. If the directors continually issue more and more shares without the permission of existing shareholders, then the proportion of shares held as a fraction of the total will of course diminish.

Public companies

Companies having a share capital, the level and type of which have satisfied the technical requirements of having those shares listed on a public share exchange.

Public companies must be designated *PLC* or *plc* in the UK. However, the fact that a company is so designated is not necessarily an indication that its shares are traded.

Private companies

Companies whose shares are not eligible for trading on a public exchange, since they do not meet certain defined characteristics. The shares may of course be bought and sold, given away as gifts (either in person or in managerial or staff incentive schemes) and inherited, but only by private contract between the parties to the transaction. Such companies are designated *Ltd* or *ltd* in the UK

Common law

A system of law-making and judgement where judges are able to interpret the application of law in individual cases, according to the laws laid down by the legislature. This gives rise to a flexible system and produces so-called 'judge-made law'. Loosely, this is a principle-based system where any behaviour is permitted provided it does not contravene the law.

Alternative systems apply legal rules for behaviour which is 'codified' in statute. The judges task is to apply the law *as written* without much scope from interpretation. Loosely, this is a rule-based system which prescribes certain types of behaviour and permits others.

Finance capitalism

An idea popularised by Rudolf Hilferding (1877–1941), a German Marxist economist in the early years of the twentieth century. The final stage of capitalism would be where entrepreneurs made money *from* money and not from the organisation of capital and labour. In more recent years the term *financial engineering* has come to assume some of the concepts associated with this idea.

Schumpeter: creative destruction

Joseph Schumpeter (1883–1950) was an Austrian economist (and, briefly, finance minister of German Austria). His analysis of capitalism held that it depended upon continual innovation and consequently, a process of 'creative destruction' where old industries, organisations and ideas are swallowed up by new ones.

The veil of incorporation

On incorporation – the process of becoming a limited company – a 'veil' is dropped between the shareholders and the company, with both becoming distinct parties. This is the price paid by the shareholders to be removed from liability for the debts of the economic entity they have just created. As a consequence they can no longer behave as if the company is their possession. They may decide to act in concert over certain issues, and even then they are bound by certain rules (established by statute) regarding the assets of the new entity – which, of course, are now no longer their assets. This veil also means that shareholders are entitled to see only certain information and have no right to demand access to the company. One of the justifications of this is that it protects all shareholders and places them on an equal footing (see Salomon v Salomon 1897).

Legal personality

On incorporation a company becomes a new legal entity – a corporate person. This enables it (a) to enter into contracts, (b) to sue and be sued and (c) to survive its original creators. It also has certain other privileges and obligations involving the compilation and retention of information.

'Corporate citizenship'

The supposition that a legal person, with rights and obligations, can also be a citizen with the rights of citizenship. A deeply flawed concept (see Chapter 2).

Ponzi schemes

Supposed investment schemes which guarantee very high returns – and are achieved solely by taking in more and more 'investments' from more and more new investors to pay out to existing investors the returns they expect and have been promised. Ivar Kreuger and Bernard Madoff are the prime exponents of this type of fraud, after the Ponzi brothers themselves.

Index

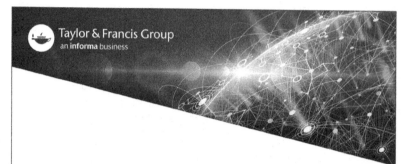

Taylor & Francis eBooks

www.taylorfrancis.com

A single destination for eBooks from Taylor & Francis
with increased functionality and an improved user
experience to meet the needs of our customers.

90,000+ eBooks of award-winning academic content in
Humanities, Social Science, Science, Technology, Engineering,
and Medical written by a global network of editors and authors.

TAYLOR & FRANCIS EBOOKS OFFERS:

A streamlined
experience for
our library
customers

A single point
of discovery
for all of our
eBook content

Improved
search and
discovery of
content at both
book and
chapter level

REQUEST A FREE TRIAL
support@taylorfrancis.com

Printed in the United States
by Baker & Taylor Publisher Services